D0383194

NATIONAL UNIVERSITY
LIBRARY   SAN DIEGO

Investigating Mathematics with Young Children

Rosemary Althouse

Teachers College, Columbia University
New York and London

NATIONAL UNIVERSITY
LIBRARY
SAN DIEGO

Published by Teachers College Press, 1234 Amsterdam Avenue,
New York, NY 10027

Copyright © 1994 by Teachers College, Columbia University

All rights reserved. No part of this publication may be reproduced
or transmitted in any form or by any means, electronic or mechanical,
including photocopy, or any information storage and retrieval system,
without permission from the publisher.

Library of Congress Cataloging-in-Publication Data

Althouse, Rosemary, 1932–
    Investigating mathematics with young children / Rosemary Althouse.
        p.   cm.
    Includes bibliographical references.
    ISBN 0–8077–3349–0 (acid-free)
    1. Mathematics — Study and teaching (Elementary)   I. Title.
QA135.5.A534   1994
372.7'044 — dc20   94-9125
                                                                   CIP

ISBN 0–8077–3349–0

Printed on acid-free paper
Manufactured in the United States of America

01 00 99 98 97 96 95 94   8 7 6 5 4 3 2 1

This book is dedicated to my young friends Sarah and Jon.

CONTENTS

PREFACE

This book is based on the 18 *Curriculum and Evaluation Standards for School Mathematics* (1989) established by the National Council of Teachers of Mathematics. Chapter 1 presents the theoretical background for the substantial advances in understanding how children learn and the current thinking about the teaching of mathematics. Chapter 2 discusses each standard and its relevance for teaching three-, four-, and five-year-old children. (Throughout, children's ages are underlined for ease of reference.)

Part II, the major portion of the book, presents activities that reflect the belief that children can learn mathematical concepts in an intellectually honest way at their level of development. Activities that reflect a transformational curriculum are included to give children opportunities to change and affect the curriculum as well as to be changed by it (Bredekamp & Rosegrant, 1992).

Throughout the book, problem solving is emphasized. Children are encouraged to formulate their own questions, find answers to those questions, and evaluate what they find.

The activities in each chapter are presented in a particular order. This does not mean, however, that you must follow that order. The interests and abilities of the group of children you are teaching will determine the direction learning takes.

ACKNOWLEDGMENTS

I wish to thank Winthrop University, the School of Education, and the Macfeat Early Childhood Laboratory School and its teachers Lori Jones, Cynthia Robinson, Mary Rix, and Mary Watson for testing my ideas. I also want to thank early childhood graduate students Betty Williams, Susan Hill, Tina Jackson, Missy Boyd, Christie Lambeth, and Karen Davis for their help in the classroom. I am indebted to kindergarten teachers Robyn Blackmon and Susan Cooper and their aide, Marilyn Price, for testing my ideas and for many of the photographs that illustrate this book. I also want to thank Sue Cauthan, principal of Great Falls Elementary, and the Chester County schools, Chester, South Carolina, for making it possible for me to work with Ms. Blackmon, Ms. Cooper, and Ms. Price. I am grateful to Jean Morse for her patience and understanding during the typing of the manuscript.

PART I

Theoretical Framework

Teaching practices in the field of mathematics have changed considerably since the early 1980s. Then, computations, drill, workbooks, and work sheets still drove the mathematics curriculum. Today, the emphasis in education is on teaching mathematics through inquiry, problem solving, and higher-order thinking skills.

Changes in the mathematics curriculum have come about as the result of many developments: the dissatisfaction of teachers with how mathematics is taught, a continuing school dropout problem, standardized tests that show children are unable to solve mathematical problems, and research that reveals how children learn and develop.

Chapter 1 discusses the theoretical findings of two significant theories of learning, *Piagetian theory* and *information processing theory*. Although these theories differ in some ways, the chapter focuses on their common features.

In 1989, the National Council of Teachers of Mathematics developed the *Curriculum and Evaluation Standards for School Mathematics*. The *Standards* are used in this book as a framework within which to plan mathematical activities for young children. They encompass the current thinking of educators and cognitive psychologists. Each standard, along with its implication for teaching mathematics to young children, is considered in Chapter 2.

TEACHING MATHEMATICS: THEORETICAL CONSIDERATIONS

Teachers of young children know that three-, four-, and five-year-olds enter preschool and kindergarten with some knowledge of mathematics. Three-year-olds understand "threeness." They will hold up three fingers when asked how old they are; say that they prefer three pieces of candy to two; and choose to put away three crayons rather than six. Four- and five-year-olds can choose 5 to 10 objects; fill a glass half-full of water; state that 10 is more than 3; and choose the larger of several boxes. Children appear to develop more and more complex mathematical understandings as they mature and interact with their environment.

During the 1970s and 1980s, research made substantial advances in understanding how children learn. The traditional view of learning, or *absorption theory*, views children as passive learners who store knowledge as a result of memorization, drill, practice, and reinforcement. Many psychologists and educators now believe that children construct their own knowledge as they interact with their environment (Hyde & Hyde, 1991; Inagaki, 1992; Schultz, Colarusso, & Strawderman, 1989; Spodek, Saracho, & Davis, 1991).

THE PIAGETIAN APPROACH

From a constructivist point of view, knowledge is created by each individual. In Piagetian theory mental structures, or *schemata*, change with intellectual development and are constructed and reconstructed gradually as children progress from one intellectual stage to another. Cognitive development is thought to flow along a continuum, with each stage built on and integrated with the previous stage (Bjorklund, 1989).

Piaget identified four stages of intellectual development: sensorimotor (ages 0–2), preoperational thought (ages 2–7), concrete operational (ages 7–11), and formal operations (ages 11–15). The ages at which individuals progress through these stages are approximate, but everyone passes through them in the same order.

Intellectual development depends on what has been learned and on the readiness of mental structures to accept new information. Piaget (1970) states, "The essential functions of intelligence consist in understanding and in inventing, in other words in building up structures by structuring reality" (p. 27). In order for structures to change, however, they must be active. This means that children must act on their environ-

3

ment mentally as well as physically. Learning is an active interaction between *thinking* children and their world.

Through acting on objects or ideas, young children often encounter discrepancies in their environment and are *motivated* to find answers that satisfy them. In this way children structure their own knowledge. Althouse (1988) explains:

> When something in the environment does not fit with what children already know, they find themselves in a state of confusion or mental imbalance—disequilibration. In order to return to a state of satisfaction or mental balance—equilibration—they are motivated to act on their environment. Children may explore objects or ideas in such a way that what they find out can be fitted into their existing conceptual framework, a process termed assimilation. During assimilation if concepts are changed or new ones formed, the process of accommodation takes place. It is through the mental processes of assimilation and accommodation that learning occurs. (pp. 3–4)

Thus, children play an important part in their own learning. When their mental structures are not ready to accept new information, they become frustrated and feel defeated. If the information is too familiar, they become bored and lose interest. When their mental structures *are* ready to receive the new information, however, children are curious and motivated to act on their environment until the information is assimilated into their conceptual framework, or the framework is altered to accommodate it, or both.

POST-PIAGETIAN THEORY

A number of researchers, sometimes referred to as post-Piagetians, have modified Piaget's conception of development to incorporate new empirical findings (Inagaki, 1992). Unlike information processing theorists, post-Piagetian researchers basically accept Piaget's constructivist point of view. Most do not, however, accept Piaget's stage theory, but believe that there are *domain-specific constraints* or *conditions* that either facilitate or hinder the acquisition of knowledge in a given area of development. In contrast, Piaget stressed the acquisition of *domain-general knowledge* that determines intellectual progress from one stage of development to another. Inagaki explains:

> Post-Piagetians have turned attention to a variety of domain-specific constraints, working in problem solving, and the acquisition of knowledge, whereas Piaget paid attention almost exclusively to domain-general (i.e., content-free) constraints of structures of thinking. (p. 120)

Domain-specific cognitive structures direct children's attention to concepts relevant to a specific cognitive domain. Due to these structures, children are more competent in some domains than in others. They will show advanced modes of reasoning in a domain they know well. They may operate at one level in a subject area and at a different level in another subject area rather than approximately at the same level in all subject areas. Among preschool and kindergarten children, for example, there are those who know more about dinosaurs than their classmates do. This familiarity with dinosaurs can be explained by a greater exposure to information about them. What children will learn about dinosaurs depends on what they already know.

Post-Piagetians believe that the other constraints affecting the construction of knowledge are innate tendencies inherent in each domain as well as sociocultural contexts, including people and artifacts. Domain-specific structures are believed to be innate, since infants and young children seem to possess them without being taught. However, as children interact with their world, these structures develop and grow. Children show more advanced modes of reasoning in the domains where they have rich experiences (Howe & Jones, 1993).

Cultural constraints mean a set of artifacts shared by people in a community or its subgroup. They include physical facilities and tools, social institutions and organizations, and symbols such as language (Inagaki, 1992). For example, children in a preschool devoid of appropriate toys and experiences may suppress their curiosity about their environment. As a result, the development of the cognitive structures necessary for structuring and restructuring knowledge may be stunted or delayed.

Social constraints include children's interactions with peers, other children, and adults. Piaget believed that children should be exposed to views other than their own in order to encounter cognitive conflict. Vygotsky (1962) pointed out that children learn more under adult guidance or in collaboration with peers than they do on their own. Post-Piagetians also believe that children can construct information more effectively when they interact with adults and peers. Children in one kindergarten were fascinated by a prism. After talking with the children about the "pretty colors," the teacher placed cut-glass perfume bottles and flat glass candy dishes on the science table. The cut glass made "pretty colors," whereas the flat glass made only a few or no "pretty colors." By including flat as well as cut glass, this teacher had introduced a discrepancy into the children's environment; what they found out about the flat glass did not fit in with what they already knew about cut glass. These children were motivated to continue their explorations with various kinds of glass in order to regain a state of equilibration. By asking questions and providing equipment for experimentation, the teacher provided adult guidance that hastened the learning experience.

The post-Piagetian conception of development has implications for the teaching of young children. It suggests that teachers can (1) choose from among many themes as long as children have prior knowledge of the topic; (2) direct and facilitate children's acquisition of knowledge by encouraging them to pursue a topic in depth; and (3) provide opportunities for children to define and solve problems through interactions with their peers.

INFORMATION PROCESSING THEORY

Information processing researchers are primarily interested in how children acquire, store, retrieve, and process information (Bjorklund, 1989). The assumption underlying this class of theories is that thinking *is* information processing. Siegler (1986) writes about these researchers:

> Rather than focusing on stages of development, they focus on the information that children represent, the processes that they use to transform the information, and the memory limits that constrain the amount of information they can represent and process. . . . A second defining characteristic of information-processing theories of development is an emphasis on precise analysis of change mechanisms. . . . Thus, information-processing theories attempt to explain both how children of given ages have come as far as they have and why they have not gone further. (p. 63)

Some concepts from information processing research that will be of interest to teachers are working memory, processing efficiency, and knowledge base.

Short-term or working memory

Information enters children's minds through their senses: sight, hearing, touch, smell, and taste. While most of it is discarded, some of it is held in children's memory for a short time and then forgotten. What happens to this information is determined primarily by how it is perceived and interpreted by children. Only the information that children pay attention to and think is important enters short-term memory (Slavin, 1988).

Short-term memory is limited by the amount of information it can store and by the rate at which information is lost from it. In *long-term memory*, it is believed, large amounts of information can be stored for indefinite periods of time. Information can enter short-term memory from long-term memory and vice versa. Because of its active nature, short-term memory is sometimes called *working memory*.

Siegler (1991) states, "It is here [in short-term memory] that information from the immediate environment and information from long-term memory are combined to perform whatever calculations are necessary" (p. 63). For example, a child said to his kindergarten teacher, "When we were talking about houses, I thought about the house I used to live in. It had a downstairs and upstairs. I had a room by myself. We had a big living room." Even in young children, events can trigger knowledge stored in long-term memory.

Processing efficiency

Information processing researchers are interested in the precise change mechanisms that enhance both short-term and long-term memory. They focus on four change mechanisms that appear to be important in cognitive development: *automation, encoding, generalization,* and *strategy construction* (Siegler, 1991). These mechanisms are the information processing counterparts of the Piagetian concepts of assimilation and accommodation; that is, they are ways of manipulating information to acquire knowledge. Although all of the change mechanisms are important to researchers, an understanding of automation is the most useful to teachers of young children.

Practice and *familiarity* are believed to enhance children's memory. Whereas controlled processes such as formulating plans and strategies require a great deal of mental effort, automatic processes, made so through practice and familiarity, do not require the individual's complete attention. These processes involve information that has been overlearned and is used even when an individual is not thinking about it. For example, in preschool and kindergarten children are expected to wash their hands before they eat a snack or lunch. After these actions are repeated many times, they become automatic, and the children no longer need to be reminded to wash their hands.

Case, Kurland, and Goldberg (1982) found that as children are mastering a developmental skill, there is an increase in processing efficiency associated with that skill. This is evident in the process of learning to ride a bicycle. A child learns to ride successfully through many trials and errors and a great deal of practice. Later, riding becomes automatic and is not forgotten.

Older children use not only more numerous but more effective strategies to help them retain information than do younger children. For example, rehearsal is used by older children as a means of remembering a task, but children under age six do not use this strategy as effectively. This may be due to their inability to understand the connection between using the strategy and remembering better. Three- and four-year-old children think that they will remember everything (Kreutzer, Leonard, & Flavell, 1975), and a large minority (30%) of five-year-olds likewise believe that they will remember everything (Flavell, Friedrichs, & Hoyt, 1970). Learning strategies seem to account for an increase in memory development in middle childhood. Young children can be taught strategies but do not always transfer them to later situations (Siegler, 1991).

Knowledge base

What children already know also affects their ability to process new information. Bjorklund (1989) states:

> It is becoming increasingly clear that what children know, or their *knowledge base*, plays an important role in how they process information. Recent

7

data indicate that the child's domain-specific knowledge, acquired continuously throughout development, accounts for many of the adult/child differences observed in cognition. (p. 59)

Price (1989) points out that learning to count and perform simple addition problems places demands on working memory. Familiarity with the information in these and other areas can make learning easier for children. He suggests that teachers can help young children excel in counting and in solving simple word problems (p. 57). For example, teachers can present familiar activities such as counting the children at lunch or in school, the number of days until Christmas, and the number of balls needed for outdoor play. Instead of being asked questions about their daily activities, children can be given simple word problems. A teacher might say, "We have six apples for lunch. Find a way to divide them so that we have enough for everyone." This is a mathematical problem that can be solved in more than one way.

SIMILARITIES AND DIFFERENCES BETWEEN THE TWO APPROACHES

Focus on the individual

Information processing researchers seek to pinpoint and explain incremental changes in cognitive development. They believe that it is these cumulative small changes rather than the qualitative leaps in development described in Piagetian stage theory that account for growth in knowledge. They also want to know why some individuals are more adept than others at learning and using specific information. For example, a kindergarten child was able to perform long division problems while most of his classmates were learning to enumerate to 20. How does one child know so much about mathematics? In precisely what ways did this child's cognitive development differ from that of his peers?

Piaget, by contrast, made no attempt to explore individual differences, because he was interested in discovering what is common to all children's learning. According to his stage theory, children cannot understand concepts that require cognitive structures not formed until a later stage of development. Piaget's stages involve qualitative as well as quantitative leaps in understanding. Post-Piagetians and information processing researchers, however, *are* interested in the differences children show in their acquisition of knowledge. Post-Piagetians explain these differences by describing restraints or conditions that hinder or enhance learning. Information processing theorists examine changes in specific mechanisms that influence learning.

Environment

The environment plays an important role in both Piagetian and information processing theory. In Piaget's theory children interact with their environment to construct and reconstruct information through a process known as equilibration. What children learn depends on the "state of readiness" of their mental schemata, which are believed to be stage-related. Post-Piagetian researchers stress the importance of domain-specific knowledge, which is determined by an individual's exposure to rich or limited experience in a specific domain of learning. In their view, what children learn about a subject is strongly influenced by what they already know.

Information processing researchers' theories emphasize the importance of the environment. What children think about and how they think about it depend on what information from the environment is stored in their short- and long-term memory. How this information is processed depends on the precise change mechanisms that work together to produce cognitive growth.

Motivation

From a Piagetian point of view, children are *motivated* to learn when they are in a state of *disequilibration*. They will act on their environment in order to return to a state of *equilibration*, or mental balance. Through the processes of *assimilation* and *accommodation*, cognitive structures are modified and new ones constructed.

An individual's first encounter with new knowledge, in the information processing model, is in the *sensory register*, which receives large amounts of information from the environment. Unless children are paying attention to and interested in a particular stimulus, it is lost or is held only very briefly in short-term memory.

Since motivation in Piagetian theory depends on the state of readiness of children's mental structures to assimilate new information from the environment, sensory input and perception are not as important. Motivation comes from inside rather than through the senses, although the particular content of what is learned will depend to some extent on the stimuli the child experiences.

Memory

Piagetian theory does not emphasize the role of memory in cognitive development. Instead, Piaget stresses the readiness of schemata to take in new information from the environment. From a Piagetian perspective, children's memory of an event undergoes developmental modifications. Children, for example, may count and recount seven objects without understanding the conservation of number. After varied experiences with objects, children count seven objects by arranging and rearranging them. They understand that the number of objects does not change unless an object is added or taken away from the group. Children's assimilating structures have evolved to the next level of development, and permit them to comprehend the activity more accurately from memory.

Information processing theorists are interested in the change mechanisms that enhance or inhibit short- and long-term memory. Automation, one of the four change mechanisms, requires *practice* and *familiarity* with specific subject matter to enhance memory.

In summary, Piagetian theory and information processing theory have much in common. Both try to identify and describe children's cognitive strengths and weaknesses at given points in their development and attempt to show how more advanced cognitive capacities grow out of earlier ones. Both emphasize the impact that existing knowledge has on the ability to process new information. Both believe that children must mentally act on information in order to "know" it. The two approaches differ in that information processing theory places more emphasis on the gradual ways in which cognitive changes occur — in what order, in what form, and for how long (Siegler, 1986) — whereas Piagetian theory emphasizes the qualitative changes in children's thinking, across many tasks, at different stages.

CURRENT TRENDS IN MATHEMATICS INSTRUCTION

The current views of educators and psychologists of how children learn have led them to criticize the way in which mathematics is taught in America's classrooms. For example, Driscoll (1988, January) comments:

> Researchers in both education and cognitive psychology have uncovered numerous flaws in the way math usually is presented to students in the classroom: flaws in shape, in sequence of topics, and most important, in the psychological assumptions about how math is learned. (pp. 1–2)

In a review of mathematical achievement data from a variety of sources over the last 20 years, Jones (1988) found evidence suggesting "a decreasing trend in average performance on tasks that require a deep understanding of mathematics, balanced by increased performances on exercises that depend on more elementary knowledge and skills" (p. 314). These findings suggest that students spend more time in the classroom on drills, work sheets, and workbooks, and less time on problem solving. If, as has been described, children structure their knowledge rather than passively receive it, they must have opportunities to act on their environment physically and mentally; to use prior knowledge to acquire new knowledge; to use methods of learning that are meaningful to them; and to become aware of and solve their own problems.

The current view of what constitutes effective mathematics instruction reflects the thinking of educators and psychologists who advocate a move away from rigid, teacher-directed programs in early childhood education to child-centered, developmentally appropriate programs. These programs take into account children's developmental levels and unique learning modes (Elkind, 1988; Ham, Perry, Corley, Taylor, &

Cooper, 1988; National Association for the Education of Young Children, 1987; National Association for the Education of Young Children and the National Association of Early Childhood Specialists in State Departments of Education, 1991; and National Association of State Boards of Education Task Force on Early Childhood Education, 1988).

Baroody (1987) describes a developmentally appropriate approach to teaching mathematics:

> Teaching mathematics is essentially a process of translating mathematics into a form children can comprehend, providing experiences that enable children to discover relationships and construct meanings, and creating opportunities to develop and exercise mathematical reasoning and problem-solving abilities. (p. 40)

In light of changing views about how children learn, of the criticisms of the current methods of teaching mathematics, of the movement away from a teacher-directed curriculum toward a more developmentally appropriate child-centered curriculum, and of the emphasis placed by educators and psychologists on the importance of problem solving, six distinct trends in the teaching of mathematics emerge:

1. Information is presented in such a way that children can use prior knowledge to reinforce and expand previous understandings and construct new ones.
2. Children are given varied and numerous opportunities to act on their environment both mentally and physically in order to define and solve problems.
3. Adults help children to define problems, seek answers, and organize information.
4. Children are encouraged to share ideas and interact with one another.
5. Information presented in the classroom is relevant to children's lives, so that they can apply it to real-world situations.
6. Children are given experiences that help them relate concepts in one content area to other concepts in the same area and to concepts in other content areas.

Based on these trends, the National Council of Teachers of Mathematics in 1989 established standards for K–12 school mathematics in the *Curriculum and Evaluation Standards for School Mathematics*. The *Standards* present a new direction for mathematics programs for children. They build on current knowledge of how children learn and develop, incorporate children's knowledge of real-life experiences with the world of mathematics, provide time for children to learn in depth, encourage children to communicate and reason mathematically, and value children's curiosity and ability to learn mathematics (Trafton & Bloom, 1990). The *Standards* state, "This document is significant because it expresses the consensus of professionals in the mathematical sciences for the direction of school mathematics in the next decade" (p. vi).

Although the *Standards* do not include three- or four-year-olds—and include five-year-olds only in the broad context of K–4—they do include topics such as estimation, measurement, number, problem solving, spatial sense, patterns, and communication. These topics and others are developmentally appropriate for children as young as age three. Topics such as fractions and decimals, statistics and probability, and computation are appropriate for older children. Several of these topics can be *introduced* to young children through preliminary concepts. Statistics cannot be understood by three-, four-, or five-year-olds, for example, but collecting and recording data can be.

Mathematical content for young children must *meet the recognized standards of the discipline*. The National Association for the Education of Young Children (NAEYC) and the National Association for Early Childhood Supervisors in State Departments of Education (NAECS/SDE) *Guidelines for Appropriate Curriculum Content and Assessment in Programs Serving Children Ages 3 Through 8* (1991) state:

> Regardless of the age of the child, educators have a responsibility to respect the knowledge base of the appropriate disciplines when formulating curriculum. In an attempt to simplify content, curriculum developers sometimes present inaccurate, misleading, or potentially confusing information. If the specific content is related to a particular discipline, then it should be as accurate as possible (although children's constructions of knowledge will not mirror adult conceptions). (p. 30)

In summary, teachers must know as much as possible about how young children learn, become more knowledgeable about the field of mathematics, and present mathematical concepts in an honest, accurate manner if they are to guide young children effectively as they explore mathematical ideas.

THE MATHEMATICS TEACHER: FROM THEORY TO PRACTICE

In most preschool and kindergarten programs, teachers capitalize on everyday happenings in the classroom. "How many children are eating a snack?" "Bring enough cups for the children at this table." "Why do you think we should put the toy in the dramatic play center?" "Put your picture in your locker." These are questions and comments that help children to develop an understanding of mathematical concepts such as one-to-one correspondence, classification, counting, and cardinal number.

That this kind of approach is widespread shows that many teachers have mathematical insight and an understanding of how children learn. Sometimes, however, in an attempt to provide mathematical experiences, teachers rely entirely on events that occur by chance, such as counting the number of acorns a child brings to school or asking children to group the leaves on the science table. Other teachers may stress learning mathematics by eliminating hands-on experiences and using only skill-oriented and highly structured, teacher-directed work sheets and workbooks. Neither approach is satisfactory if teachers want children to construct, clarify, and integrate mathematical ideas by interacting with their environment.

Mathematical experiences must be carefully planned. Teachers not only must understand how children learn, they also must know and respect mathematics as a discipline. They should strive to understand which mathematical concepts are developmentally appropriate for the children they teach, and to relate these concepts to one another and to other curriculum areas. Teachers must guide, not direct, children's learning so that they can construct their own mathematical knowledge. Kamii (1982) states, "The task of the teacher is to encourage the child's thinking in his own way, which is difficult because [most] of us were trained to get children to produce right answers" (p. 26).

THE NCTM *STANDARDS*

This chapter is based on the belief that many of the concepts in the *Curriculum and Evaluation Standards for School Mathematics* (1989) of the National Council of Teachers of Mathematics are adaptable to the teaching of mathematics in preschool and kindergarten. The *Standards* state, "We believe that similar standards need to be developed for both preschool and those beyond high school" (p. 7). The *Standards* for grades K–4 students stem from the belief that mathematics is a sense-making experience and that children should be active, not passive, participants in learning. Trafton and Bloom (1990) state:

> It [the NCTM *Standards*] builds upon current knowledge about their development and their learning. It links children's intuitive mathematical insights and knowledge with the world of mathematics by incorporating real-world contexts and their everyday experiences and language. It recognizes the complexities of mathematical learning by providing time for children to develop sound understandings and to learn to communicate and reason mathematically. It also values having children retain their mathematical curiosity and their belief that they can learn and make sense out of mathematics. (p. 482)

Because they are so central to the material in this chapter, the K–4 *Standards* are reproduced here:

1. *Mathematics as Problem Solving* [Young children define and solve their own mathematical problems. Problem solving is stressed in the context of each Standard.]
2. *Mathematics as Communication* [Young children communicate mathematical understandings verbally and in writing.]
3. *Mathematics as Reasoning* [Young children "think" about mathematics in real-life situations and apply what they know to solving mathematical problems.]
4. *Mathematical Connections* [Young children are exposed to the relationships between and among subject areas rather than to purely mathematical topics.]
5. *Estimation* [Young children learn to use estimation as a way of evaluating their answers to mathematical problems.]
6. *Number Sense and Numeration* [Young children use concepts such as one-to-one correspondence, counting, cardinal number, and classifying in real-life situations.]
7. *Concepts of Whole Number Operations* [Young children are not ready for formal addition and subtraction; however, they can understand processes such as combining and separating objects and terms such as *more, less,* and *the same as.*]
8. *Whole Number Computation* [Young children are not ready for formal addition, subtraction, division, or multiplication.]
9. *Geometry and Spatial Sense* [Young children are exposed to topographical terms such as *near, close to, next to,* etc. They learn the concept of shape and the names of a few geometrical shapes. They are not ready for formal Euclidean geometry.]
10. *Measurement* [Young children use nonstandard units to measure

objects. They explore the relationship between the size of the unit and the resulting measurements.]

11. *Statistics and Probability* [Children can gather and record data from meaningful everyday experiences. Young children do not understand the concepts of statistics or probability.]

12. *Fractions and Decimals* [Young children are not ready for a formal study of fractions or decimals.]

13. *Patterns and Relationships* [Young children can identify patterns in their environment and make their own patterns with concrete objects. They are able to show patterns symbolically through drawings and paintings.] (p. 15)

HOW CHILDREN LEARN MATHEMATICAL CONCEPTS

What follows is a review of the literature related to young children's mathematical thinking, organized according to each K–4 *Standard* and its recommendations for teaching young children.

Problem solving

During the 1980s, students in most classrooms, including some children as young as <u>four</u> or <u>five</u>, were taught mathematics through work sheets, workbooks, <u>drills</u>, and practice. This approach came about as a reaction to the open education classrooms of the 1970s and as a result of parental pressure on the schools. Consequently, children in classrooms across the nation were not asked to think about or solve mathematical problems for themselves.

Problem solving is an internal process in which children create new mental relationships as they interact with their environment and relate new understandings to previous ones (Dixon & Chalmers, 1990). In order to solve problems, children must first be able to *identify* them. Identifying a problem is being aware that something in the environment does not fit in with what is already known. The second step in problem solving is *seeking answers* to the problem, the third step is *selecting effective processes* needed to solve the problem, and the last step is *choosing a solution* to the problem that is satisfactory to the individual.

In early childhood, problem solving involves physical as well as mental action. When children manipulate objects, they learn the physical properties inherent in the objects themselves. Piaget defined this kind of knowledge as *physical knowledge*. *Logico-mathematical knowledge* occurs when children create or invent relationships between and among objects. In order to create relationships, children need to handle objects and observe how they react. If children are to solve problems, teachers must provide materials for children to act on because "Young children think better when they are physically acting on objects" (Williams & Kamii, 1986, p. 26).

In the late 1980s, as the educational reform movement focused on restructuring the schools, educators became interested in the concept of *cooperative learning*, in which children work in groups and learn from their interactions. Early childhood educators have always believed that the quality of social interactions determines children's self-image and belief in themselves as learners. Research in a series of cognitive conflict studies of young children ages <u>five</u> to <u>nine</u> is relevant to preschool and kindergarten teachers. Tudge and Caruso (1988) found that solving problems by cognitive conflict was more successful when children shared a common goal and had different perspectives on reaching the goal. They offer several suggestions for encouraging children to interact and share different perspectives during cooperative learning:

> Plan activities in which children have a shared goal.
> Choose goals that are intrinsically interesting to the children.
> Children should be able to achieve their goal by means of their own activities.
> The results of the child's actions should be both visible and immediate. (p. 50)

Tudge and Caruso's suggestions can be applied to teaching preschool and kindergarten children. Teachers can promote cooperative learning by helping children to:

1. *Plan together.* Children can, for example, decide how to build a structure, discuss what is needed for a snack, or decide what props to use for a dramatization.
2. *Set up their own objectives.* Planning a grocery store, finding props to act out a familiar story, and preparing snacks are activities of interest to young children that can be carried out by them.
3. *Achieve goals by their own actions.* Teachers can provide materials or encourage children to find or develop their own materials. Children building a tall building, for example, can use boxes rather than heavy blocks.
4. *Become aware of the results of their actions.* When children see the results of their ideas, they are able to change their strategies. Children who see that the same objects placed on either side of an equal-arm balance do not change the balance can direct their attention to the placement of the fulcrum.

Children in developmentally appropriate classrooms often identify and solve problems without assistance from adults. One <u>three-year-old</u>, for example, made several attempts to stand up animals in a carpeted area of the classroom. Finally he made an animal stand by pushing its feet into the rug. He immediately did the same thing with the other animals. He made no comments to the teacher, but said to another child, "Look, my animals are standing on the rug."

When children show by their actions or verbalizations that they are unable to identify problems, teachers can ask open-ended questions such as "Do you have enough napkins for each child?" or "Why do you think your building fell down?" Teachers must also create problem-solving situations by challenging children's thinking. Placing an assortment of objects on a table and saying, "Put the objects together that are alike in some way" is an example of challenging children by asking them to set up their own classification system.

If children lose interest or become frustrated in their attempts to solve problems, teachers can make suggestions or model behaviors for them. In one kindergarten, children who blew hard and fast into straws failed in their attempts to blow bubbles. They became frustrated with bubble blowing. In order to show the children a way to blow bubbles successfully, the teacher blew gently and slowly into a straw. After watching the teacher, the children were able to blow bubbles by imitating her behavior.

Introducing discrepancies — events that do not fit in with what children already know or expect — is one of the best ways to create problem-solving opportunities. One teacher placed small but heavy pieces of wood and large but light pieces of wood near an equal-arm balance. The children predicted that the large pieces of wood would be heavier than the small pieces. They were surprised to see that the small pieces of wood were heavier than the large pieces. The children decided that small objects could be heavier than large ones. Teachers must allow children to determine whether they are satisfied with the answers to their problems.

Most important, teachers must trust children to learn through their own efforts. In my experience, teachers' lack of belief in children's ability to think and their desire to give children "right" answers have often destroyed possibilities for problem solving.

Communication

Teachers often encourage children to express themselves verbally, but may ignore the possibilities for "mathematics talk" inherent in children's drawings and models. A number of theories have been used to explain children's art. Among these is the *cognitive theory*, which assumes children draw what they know. Seefeldt (1987) explains, "As children gain in understanding, grow, and have more experiences, they increase their fund of concepts; likewise, their drawings and paintings increase in detail, complexity, and accuracy" (p. 186).

Representing mathematics through writing, painting, and drawing helps children to think about ideas, events, and relationships. Although most young children do not spell or form letters correctly, they can represent their mathematical ideas through scribbles, letterlike forms, or inventive spelling.

Teachers should encourage children to use letterlike forms or to dictate what they want written. *Dictation* and *inventive spelling* are part of the *whole-language approach* to teaching reading. Whole-language learning involves strategies that allow children to construct their own learning from present and past experiences (Gothard & Russell, 1990). In inventive spelling, children invent spellings that reflect the way particular words sound to them.

Language experiences that involve written and verbal expression are appropriate ways of encouraging children to express mathematical understandings. Whitin, Mills, and O'Keefe (1990) describe how one teacher in a first-grade transitional program used what children knew about language and number to improve the mathematics program. The children in this classroom included in their drawings words and numerals conveying mathematical ideas. During a discussion of growing and losing teeth, the children drew pictures of their mouths with teeth missing. One child wrote the numerals 6–1–5–1 to show that her sister had six teeth, lost one, then had five, and grew one back. Other children expressed their mathematical understandings through similar pictures. The entire mathematics program was built around stories and strategies to support mathematical literacy. The authors state, "After all, mathematics is a language too. It is a communication system that we use to explore and expand our knowledge of the world" (p. 10).

Older preschool and kindergarten children are capable of recording future as well as past events. At-risk children in a kindergarten classroom drew pictures to show their plans for making construction toys. Not only could they draw their plans, but they could describe in detail what they were going to do. One child drew plans for a tall box-like construction. When he could not find a box exactly like the one he had drawn, he put a cross mark through the box on his plan (Althouse, 1988).

Teachers have many opportunities to further children's mathematical understandings through both verbal and written expression. One kindergarten teacher asked children to dictate birthday stories. These stories illustrate children's use of mathematical language to describe important events. One story read:

> My birthday is today.
> I am six years old.
> I have six candles on my cake.
> My mother is coming to school.
> My sister is two years old.
> My brother is big. He is 12 years old.

Reasoning

In Piaget's theory of development, children's ability to reason is limited by their egocentric view of the world. When Piaget speaks of children as being egocentric, he means that they are capable of seeing the world from only one vantage point—their own—and tend to be unaware of other ways of looking at the world. They do not feel that they must justify their actions or thoughts, and they are unable to take the needs of a listener into consideration. Between the ages of four and seven, children become less egocentric (Gallagher & Reid, 1991). Although preoperational children (ages two to seven) are more egocentric than concrete operational children (ages seven to twelve), post-Piagetian research indicates that young children are capable, in certain situations, of taking the perspective of another by age three or four.

One of the criticisms made of cognitive research is that it is usually conducted in a structured laboratory setting rather than in a natural classroom setting (Bjorklund, 1989). Using a more naturalistic method, Revelle, Wellman, and Karabenick (1985) observed children playing with adults in two play settings. The adults asked children ambiguous questions ("Bring me the cup," when there were four cups) and logical questions ("Bring me a shovel from the sandpile"). Three- and four-year-old children discriminated between the ambiguous and logical questions and made appropriate responses for solving the problems. Shatz and Gelman (1973) found that four-year-olds modified their voice and discourse according to whether they were talking to adults, children their age, or two-year-olds. When they talked to two-year-olds, they used shorter sentences and a different tone of voice.

Four- and five-year-olds are aware that they reason. They know that thinking, remembering, dreaming, and knowing are all mental processes that require the use of their brain. Even three-year-olds are aware that thinking occurs in the brain and that the brain is in the head. In one nursery school, a three-year-old who was measuring a block with coffee stirrers was asked, "How long is this block?" He answered, "Two stirrers." "How do you know?" asked the teacher. "My brain told me," he replied.

If children are to reason mathematically, they must feel confident to trust and express their own thinking. Their explanations may be only partially correct, but what is important is that they feel comfortable *thinking* about their thinking. Explanations of their thinking must be accepted by teachers. As Resnick (1989) writes:

> We used to think of errors as just mistakes, something to be gotten rid of, but now we see that errors are frequently the result of a person's trying hard to make sense of something. It follows that teachers may not always want to teach the rules and "tricks of the trade" that get rid of errors,

because they might be getting rid of the clues they need in order to follow their students' thinking. (p. 15)

Mathematical connections

In developmentally appropriate preschools and kindergartens, learning is not segregated into separate compartments. Katz and Chard (1989) state, "The stream of daily life experiences does not occur in categories such as science and history. The content of experience is more like events or topics than discrete disciplines" (p. 6). When teaching by a topic, unit, or project approach, teachers should make every attempt to relate one mathematical experience to another. They should also make mathematics relevant to children's lives and to other disciplines.

The National Association for the Education of Young Children and National Association of Early Childhood Supervisors in State Departments of Education *Guidelines* (1991) advocate an integrated curriculum that helps children make connections between home and school and between different subject matter areas. A unit on "Ourselves," for example, can be planned so that children compare the lengths of their arms, legs, and other body parts (mathematics), talk about their families (social studies), learn to take care of their bodies (science), and listen to stories about children like themselves (language arts).

Estimation

Children in primary grades often have difficulty making effective estimations because they are too concerned with getting the "right answer." Baroody (1987) states, "They lack the (a) prerequisite skills and concepts, (b) estimation strategies themselves, or (c) flexibility to engage in an inexact but thoughtful problem-solving process" (p. 238). Estimation is a skill that should be taught as early as nursery school. It is a natural way to introduce mathematical concepts, and if children are encouraged to estimate first, later they will be more interested in getting precise answers to questions (Schultz, Colarusso, & Strawderman, 1989).

Teachers can help young children to use estimation and to think of it as a problem-solving process. Some questions teachers can ask children as they work with materials and engage in classroom activities are: "Are you planning to build a short or tall building? How many blocks will you need?" "Do you want a small or large piece of paper to make a hat for the doll?" "How many pieces of masking tape do you need to hang up your picture?" and "How long must the string be to reach across the room?" Whenever possible, children should be encouraged to compare their estimations with the final results.

As children mature and have many experiences with estimation, their ability to estimate becomes more accurate. A four-year-old asked her teacher how long it would be before they went outdoors. The teacher answered, "We'll go in ten minutes." Becky asked, "Is that long?" Her teacher asked, "What do you think?" Becky replied, "I think short." A three-year-old overheard the conversation and said, "Ten minutes is too long to wait."

Number sense and numeration

In Piagetian theory, *cardinal number* or "how many" is a synthesis of *one-to-one correspondence, conservation of number,* and *class inclusion.* Children must assign a number name (one-to-one correspondence) to each item in a set and understand that the last number of the last object includes all the other items (class inclusion). Counting meaningfully also depends on the conservation of number. When children realize that the number of objects in a group remains the same regardless of how the objects are arranged, they understand conservation of number (Kamii, 1982). Most children understand conservation of number and class inclusion by age six or seven. A few children conserve number and understand class inclusion at as early an age as five and-a-half or six.

Counting and one-to-one correspondence. Price (1989) states:

> Studies of experts have shown that being an expert at solving the problems of a domain almost invariably requires one to possess knowledge unique to that domain. Two such forms of mathematical knowledge are *skill at counting* and *strategies for solving simple word problems.* (p. 55)

He feels that teachers who know how counting skills develop can better appreciate children's counting efforts even when their counting is not "correct" in a conventional sense.

When preschool children are given *small* sets of objects to count, children as young as three can count four objects correctly. Many kindergarten children can count by 1 (one-to-one correspondence), use counting words in a consistent sequence (the stable order principle), and realize that the last word in the counting sequence represents the total amount (cardinal number). They also know that a set can be counted beginning with any object in the set (Gelman & Gallistel, 1978). Fuson, Richards, and Briars (1982) found that nursery-school children could not "count on" beginning with numbers other than 1, but that most kindergarten children could "count on" from other numbers.

Kamii (1985) points out that children may not have the underlying mental structures needed to count. Teachers are very familiar with young children who can mentally order three objects but have difficulty counting six or eight objects. They often assign a number name to more than one object or skip an object as they count. These children do not mentally put the objects into some kind of order. Children may be able to count objects but may point to the last object counted when they are asked to show how many objects are in a set. These children may not understand the concept of *class inclusion*. If there are seven objects, 6 is included in 7, 5 is included in 6, and so on. Kamii (1982) suggests that teachers of young children spend less time on counting and more time on one-to-one correspondence and the comparison of groups of objects. When children create their own sets for comparison, learning is more meaningful. Teachers, for example, who ask, "Do we have enough chairs for the children?" encourage them to compare the chairs with the number of children. This question can be solved by counting each set, but also by placing the chairs and children into one-to-one correspondence.

In summary, research indicates that children as young as three have number sense. Three-, four-, and five-year-olds can count small numbers of objects, while some children from ages five to six have the mental structures needed to understand class inclusion. This does not mean that teachers should try to teach class inclusion to young children. If the mental structures needed for understanding class inclusion are not present, children may become confused or memorize correct answers for problems they do not understand.

Children in nursery school and kindergarten are involved in one-to-one situations throughout the day. They choose cups for juice, set the table for snacktime, or count the blocks in their buildings or the children in a group. Teachers can also plan activities that require children to use one-to-one correspondence and compare groups of objects. One teacher said to two four-year-old boys, "Please put the chairs in the center for group time." She did not remind them of the number of children in school. The boys placed several chairs in the center. They were soon occupied and several children were standing and complaining, "I don't have a chair." The boys brought additional chairs for the children. They didn't count the chairs, but continued to make a one-to-one correspondence between children and chairs until each child had a chair. They looked at the children sitting in the chairs and said, "We don't need any more chairs." One child said, "*You* don't have chairs." Each boy hurriedly found a chair for himself. The teacher had worded her question wisely so that, in order to solve the problem, the boys had to use one-to-one correspondence and compare sets. With the help of the other children, they were able to solve the problem themselves.

Conservation of number. In a Piagetian task, children are given two identical rows of 8 to 10 objects, with each object in each row placed parallel to the corresponding object in the other row. They are asked whether the rows have the same numbers of objects. If they agree that the numbers are the same, the objects in one of the rows are spread out. The children are then asked whether the rows are still the same. Most children between ages three and six will say that the row with the objects farther apart is longer (Copeland, 1988). They are fooled by perception because the row "looks" as if it had more objects. These children are said to be nonconservers of number because they do not realize that the number of objects remains the same regardless of the arrangement. Researchers have found that when the number of objects is small and the questions are worded differently, children around age five can conserve number. Gelman (1972) found that children between ages three-and-a-half and five could conserve number when two to three objects were involved.

Ginsburg (1980) describes his research indicating that children from ages three to six have a concept of "more" and "less." Pennies were placed on two identical dishes, five pennies on one dish and seven pennies on the other dish. Children were asked to point to the dish with more pennies. Children as young as three were able to point to the correct dish. When large numbers of pennies were used, children had difficulty with the problem. Although children do have trouble with Piagetian tasks, they have strengths in other areas, such as understanding "more" and "less."

Teachers should not attempt to teach conservation of number directly, but they can give children experiences that help them to realize that materials do not increase or decrease in quantity when their appearance changes (Leeb-Lundberg, 1989). Rearranging block constructions, pulling clay apart and pushing it back together, rearranging and counting objects, and taking things apart and putting them back together are activities that demonstrate conservation principles.

Classification. There are three main stages of classification. The first is *sorting* and occurs when children put like objects together (about age two). The second, *multiple classification*, occurs when children understand that an object may belong to more than one group. A red wooden block can belong in the group of red objects and in the group of wooden objects. Most children understand multiple classification between ages six and seven. The third level, *class inclusion*, is the ability to understand that the whole is greater than its parts. If a set includes boys and girls, it contains more children than it does either boys or girls. Before age six or seven, the concept of the whole, *children*, is lost when the parts, *boys* and *girls*, are considered (Copeland, 1988).

When the number of objects is small and questions on Piagetian tasks are reworded, younger children too may show an understanding of class inclusion. Markman and Seibert (1976) reported a higher level of performance when experimenters' questions involved *collections*, groups of items related on the basis of part/whole relations rather than class inclusion relations. In other words, it is easier for children to relate to boys and girls as belonging to a kindergarten class (a specific collection) than to boys and girls belonging to the category children (class inclusion).

Children in preschool and kindergarten sort objects when, for example, they put those that go together on shelves or in boxes of similar

23

objects. All kinds of collections are made by children. The science table may have a collection of nuts, the house center a collection of doll clothes, and the block center a collection of toy people. Children may be asked questions such as "Do we have more acorns or more nuts?" "Are there more dresses or more doll clothes in the house center?" and "Do you have more daddies or more toy people in your block house?" Teachers can help children to understand the relationship of the whole and its parts by talking about the relationships between and among familiar objects. Children may be asked questions such as "How many boys are there in school? How many girls? Do we have more kindergarten children or more boys in our class?"

Ordinal number. Ordinal number answers the question "Which one?" Is it the first, the second, or the tenth object? In order to understand ordinal number, children must first order objects by comparing them to some criterion, such as length, color, or size. Most children can, by age six or seven, order 8 to 10 objects. Preschool children can order 3 to 4 objects while kindergarten children can order 6 to 10 (Kamii, 1982). The teacher's responsibility in helping children to develop ordering skills is to be alert to everyday experiences that lend themselves to ordering, such as comparing large and small objects, long and short objects, and dark and light colors. Teachers should also plan ordering activities such as photographing classroom events and encouraging children to order the resulting pictures.

Writing numerals. Children as young as age four may write numerals and letters within the same word (inventive spelling). Gradually, they begin to associate number names with counting objects. They may write a numeral to show their age, the number of days until a trip, or the number of pets at home. Teachers should encourage children to use written symbols (numerals) in their drawings and paintings (Baker & Baker, 1991; Whitin, Mills, & O'Keefe, 1990). When children write, teachers can tell them to begin at the top and pull down to make letters and numerals. In my experience this procedure has been very helpful to children.

One of the best ways to determine how much children understand about number is to ask, "Can you find a way to show me _____?" Children may write numerals, draw figures, or count out the required number of objects. One child handed his teacher six balls of clay and a pair of scissors to show "seven."

Whole number operations: Preliminary concepts

It is developmentally inappropriate to teach addition and subtraction in preschool and kindergarten (National Association for the Education of Young Children, 1987). There are, however, concepts associated with addition and subtraction word problems that can be introduced when similar problems arise in the classroom.

Information processing theory has revealed that the demand on *working memory* is often what makes mathematical problems difficult. Familiarity with information improves working memory and raises performance. Studies show that skill at counting and strategies for solving word problems help children to become more expert at solving mathematical problems. In Price's (1989) opinion, many young children can solve addition and subtraction word problems without formal instruction. He describes four basic classes of addition and subtraction problems: *join* problems, *separate* problems, *combine* problems, and *compare* problems (p. 56).

Although these types of problems are introduced in first grade, the situations they represent sometimes occur in preschool and kindergarten classrooms. The following are examples of classroom scenarios and ways in which teachers can guide children's thinking:

Join problems: Jimmy was building a zoo with blocks. He said, "I have seven blocks. Someone give me some blocks." Jane handed him four blocks. His teacher asked, "How many blocks do you have now?" Jimmy counted the blocks and said, "Nine." Jane said, "No, there are eleven." The teacher said, "Jimmy, can you think of a way to arrange your blocks so that you can count them easily?" Jimmy arranged the blocks in a row and counted 11.

Separate problems: A teacher heard two children arguing about the ownership of several small rocks. Susan said to Alice, "I had three of the rocks. Give them to me." Alice counted her rocks and said, "I only have eight, but you can have your three back." She gave Susan three rocks and said, "Now I don't have as many." The teacher said, "You had eight rocks and you gave Alice three. How many do you have now?" Alice looked at the rocks in her hand, counted mentally, and said, "Five."

Combine problems: This kind of problem is very familiar to young children. At a snack table there were two boys and four girls. The teacher asked, "How many children are at the table?" One child counted six children. The teacher asked, "How many boys are at the table?" The child answered, "Two boys." She asked, "How many girls?" He answered, "Four." Another child said, "I know it's six 'cause four and two are six."

Compare problems: These problems are difficult for young children to solve and often require one-to-one correspondence if children are to find the answers. A teacher asked a child to bring enough napkins for the lunch table. Bill brought napkins and placed them on the table in random order. He said, "I think there are too many." The teacher asked, "Do you have as many napkins as you need?" Bill said, "I don't know." Then he made a one-to-one correspondence between the napkins and the chairs. He said, "I had too many napkins. Now I have enough."

There are many other "word problem" situations that teachers can help children solve by asking them questions, encouraging them to count concrete materials, or helping them to make one-to-one correspondence between two sets of objects to determine the larger set.

Whole number computation

As stated in the previous section, preschool and kindergarten children do not have the mathematical understandings needed for formal addition, subtraction, multiplication, and division.

Geometry and spatial sense

Topology. Children's first experiences with shapes are topological in nature. In the mathematics of topology, figures are not considered fixed or rigid. Closed figures, such as squares, circles, and triangles, are equivalent topologically because they may be pulled or squeezed to form one another (Copeland, 1988; Schultz, Colarusso, & Strawderman, 1989). Young children's understanding of topology may explain why many three- and four-year-olds draw circles when they are given squares to copy. It may also explain their fascination with circles — drawing circles, talking about circles, and playing with circles.

The first topological relationship is *proximity*, or the closeness of objects. The second is the *separation* of objects from other objects or the parts of an object from the object. The third is *order*, the placement of objects; and the fourth is *enclosure*, the surroundings of objects (Schultz, Colarusso, & Strawderman, 1989).

Often children's drawings and paintings reveal an understanding of topological relations. In describing their pictures children may use topological terminology such as *in–out*, *on–off*, and *inside–outside*. Related terms such as *left–right*, *closer–farther*, and *toward–away* also reveal an understanding of topology. Teachers can also judge children's spatial understandings by observing their placement of objects in space. Are the figures on a baseline? Are they placed in the proper relationships to other objects? Are peoples' features in the correct order and surrounded by the outline of their faces? Teachers should remember that children during the early preschool years represent people and things with circles and straight lines.

Teachers of three- and four-year-old children should question children about topological relationships as they work with materials: "Is the dog inside or outside the barn?" "Is the tree near the house or near the fence?" "Are the cars in the garage?" "Are the rooms separated from each other? How?"

Perspective. Perspective is a difficult concept for young children. In a Piagetian task, a cardboard range of mountains is set on a table in front of children who are then asked to walk around the mountains, viewing them from all sides. The children are given several pictures and are asked to select the one that shows what they see from their point of view. Then a doll is moved from one point of view to another. Children are asked to pick the picture showing the doll's new point of view. Not until age seven or eight do children correctly identify the doll's angle of view (Pulaski, 1971).

In a simplified version of Piaget's spatial task, children are presented with the task of identifying a doll's perspective of a three-dimensional display. The display contains objects familiar to children, such as a lake with a sailboat. The children are asked to rotate an exact duplicate of the display to indicate what the doll sees. Three- and four-year-old children are able to choose the correct display 80 to 90 percent of the time. During the later preschool years, children can describe the exact position of objects viewed by the doll (Borke, 1975). It seems that children find it much easier to indicate another person's point of view when asked to turn a three-dimensional display than when asked to select a picture from a group of pictures. Scenes depicting familiar objects are easier to identify than scenes with less familiar objects.

One of the best ways to help children understand perspective is to discuss significant landmarks and their locations. The dramatic play center, for example, is next to the block center, and the jungle gym is behind the paved riding area.

Teachers can also introduce children to different views of their surroundings. While children are playing, they can take photographs of different areas of the classroom and playground. Even when children are in the photographs, they sometimes have problems identifying the locations shown in the pictures.

Euclidean shapes. Children proceed from topological and projective ideas to an understanding of Euclidean shapes. Teachers should first provide experiences for children with *three-dimensional* shapes such as building blocks and construction toys. Gradually, teachers can move to *two-dimensional* shapes such as puzzle pieces and construction paper and then to *one-dimensional* shapes such as string and alphabet letter parts (Schultz, Colarusso, & Strawderman, 1989; Copeland, 1988).

In order for children to construct concepts about shapes such as squares and triangles, they should handle the objects and trace their outlines with their fingers, beginning and ending at the same point. Copeland (1972) states, "'Drawing' marks the transition from visual perception to idea-motor representation and the ability to draw is a measure of the ability to represent a given shape" (p. 24). Children typically draw circles at about age three, and squares and triangles at about age five (Althouse, 1981). The ability to recognize a shape slightly precedes the ability to draw it.

Three- and four-year-olds can be exposed to circles in a variety of ways—by placing tops on round containers, playing ring toss, standing in a circle, or making circles with yarn, string, and pipe cleaners, for example. Five-year-olds should learn about all kinds of Euclidean shapes such as triangles, squares, rectangles, pentagons, and octagons.

Schultz, Colarusso, and Strawderman (1989) caution teachers to avoid naming shapes until children can pronounce the names of shapes and use them meaningfully. They state:

> Teachers can listen to the labels children give for different shapes and use those labels to define the formal terms. . . .
>
> Parts of these objects should also be named with language available to the child. Some examples are corner for *angle*, point for *vertex*, line for *edge*, bottom for *base*, and so on. (pp. 284–285)

Measurement

Length. *Conservation of length* usually is not understood by children until they are age six-and-a-half to seven (Dutton & Dutton, 1991). Young children do not understand that the length of an object does not change when it is moved along another object being measured. In a Piagetian task, children are given two sticks of the same length and asked to place them parallel to each other. Once they agree that the sticks are the same length, one stick is moved forward, away from the other stick. Young children think the stick that has been moved is longer. They do not realize that the length of the stick is unchanged (Copeland, 1988).

Gelman (1969) taught five-year-olds to conserve by training them to attend to the correct dimensions in Piagetian tasks of number and length. Bjorklund (1989) cautions that while training and transfer effects are impressive, they have been conducted in the laboratory rather than in the school or classroom. Recent books on the teaching of mathematics in early childhood education (Dutton & Dutton, 1991; Schultz, Colarusso, & Strawderman, 1989; Hyde & Hyde, 1991) suggest that teachers introduce linear measurement by encouraging children to compare two familiar objects to discover which one is longer. Later, nonstandard units may be directly compared by aligning a unit (for example, a paper clip, a coffee stirrer, or a dowel) along an object.

Teachers should encourage children to use nonstandard units of measurement rather than standard units such as rulers and yardsticks. Children enjoy measuring themselves and each other with long strips of paper. Once children become interested in measurement, they can measure and compare the measurements of objects in their classroom. One child reported that his block construction was 6 coffee stirrers, 1 popsicle stick, and 4 dowels long.

Area. The ability to *conserve area* appears at about age seven to seven-and-a-half (Dutton & Dutton, 1991). During a Piagetian task children are shown two same-size sheets of green paper with a toy cow placed on each. They are told to pretend that the paper is grass for the cows to eat. Then they are asked, "Which cow has more grass to eat? or do the cows have the same amount?" Typically, children answer that the cows have the same amount of grass to eat. Then a block representing a barn is placed on each paper and the question is repeated. Again the answer is typically that the cows have the same amount to eat. A second block is placed in each field, but in one field the block is far from the first, whereas in the other field it is placed adjacent to the other block. The question is repeated, "Which cow has more grass to eat? or do they both have the same amount?" The nonconservers say that the cow in the field with the adjacent blocks has more grass to eat. In reality, it simply looks that way (Wadsworth, 1984).

Children learn the concepts of surface and area by understanding that objects have a *covering property*. Dutton and Dutton (1991) state, "Two kinds of relationships can be discovered: equivalence (covers as much as) and inequivalence (covers more, most, less, least)" (p. 78). Children's first experiences with area involve covering the surface of one object with smaller objects and covering one object with another object. Is the object bigger than, smaller than, or the same size as the other object?

Children also have experiences with area when they draw around their bodies on the floor and see how much space they cover. Teachers can give children opportunities to draw around parts of their bodies, compare the amounts of space various parts cover, and draw spaces to fit parts of their bodies.

Volume. Children do not conserve volume until about age eight-and-a-half to nine (Schultz, Colarusso, & Strawderman, 1989; Dutton & Dutton, 1991). In a Piagetian task, children are shown two containers of equal size and shape filled to the same level with water. They are asked whether the glasses contain the same amount of liquid. When children agree that the amounts are the same, the water in one glass is poured into a tall, thin glass. Children are again asked whether the containers have the same amount of liquid. Fooled by perception, young children typically say that the tall container has more liquid (Wadsworth, 1984). Although young children cannot be expected to understand the difference between *volume* and *capacity*, early childhood teachers should understand the distinction. Capacity refers to the amount of space within a container and volume refers to the amount of space a container occupies (Dutton & Dutton, 1989).

Children can fill various shaped containers with sand and water. They can then make comparisons between and among the containers. Teachers can ask questions such as: "Which container holds more water?" "How do you know?" "If you want to make a big sand cake, which container will you choose?" "How many cups of water do you think it will take to fill this container?"

Quantity. In order to *conserve quantity*, children must understand that the *mass* of an object remains the same no matter what shape it takes. Although the shape of a ball of clay may change, its mass remains the same if nothing is added and nothing is taken away from it. Most children do not attain conservation of quantity until around age eight or nine (Dutton & Dutton, 1991; Charlesworth & Lind, 1990).

Although young children do not conserve quantity, they can explore mass by pulling, separating, and putting back together objects such as clay and construction toys. Children can hold an object in each hand and estimate which object has the greater mass. Later they can check their predictions with an equal-arm balance. When referring to the mass of an object, children will probably use the term *weight*. This is acceptable, and teachers should not correct them.

Weight. There are terms related to measurement that are important for teachers to know but are not used with preschool and kindergarten children. Schultz, Colarusso, and Strawderman (1989) state, "Technically mass is the correct term for the study of measurement but the familiar terms of *weight* and *weigh* were dominant" (p. 320). Although children typically do not conserve weight until age nine or ten, they often lift objects and say, "See I'm strong. It's heavy, but I can lift it" or "This is easy to lift. It's light."

Weight-related terms that children use in making comparisons between and among objects are *heavy, light, big, little, heaviest, lightest, biggest, smallest, lighter than,* and *heavier than.* Young children are fascinated by equal-arm balances and enjoy comparing the masses of objects. They will refer to mass as weight and compare objects as the heavier one and the lighter one.

Time. Children do not conserve time until age seven or eight and do not completely understand time until age eight or nine (Dutton & Dutton, 1991). Young children think that they control time. When they move fast, time passes quickly, and when they move slowly, time moves less rapidly. Since they believe that time is related to their activities, they do not comprehend standard units of time measurement.

Vukelich and Thornton (1990) explain children's understanding of historical time as follows: Young children—three- to five-year-olds—understand sequential time when it is related to activities in their daily lives. They also know that some members of their families are older than others.

Charlesworth and Lind (1990) have analyzed children's experiences with time by distinguishing three ways time enters their lives. *Personal time* refers to children's own past, present, and future. Young children have more trouble conceiving of the past and future than of the present. *Social time* refers to what children do or the sequence of events in their lives. Teachers can help children envision social time by talking with them about the sequence of events in the school day — for example, hanging up coats, having playtime, and then eating snacks. *Cultural time* refers to time that is measured by clocks and calendars (pp. 230–231). Teachers can help children become familiar with the language of time by referring to clocks, calendars, and watches. Children enjoy playing with all kinds of timers, such as 60-minute timers, hourglasses, and 1- and 3-minute sand timers.

Statistics and probability

Only an introduction to *gathering and recording data* is appropriate for preschool and kindergarten children. They can gather data and record them in concrete, picture, symbol, or written form. Whitin, Mills, and O'Keefe (1990) have shown how children in a transitional first-grade classroom used graphs throughout the school year. The authors divide graphing experiences into four categories:

1. Integrating graphs into the daily life of the classroom. [How many children have blue eyes? brown eyes? green eyes? etc.]
2. Encouraging personal surveys. [How many times this week did I play in the house center? the block center? the art center? etc.]
3. Constructing graphs to make classroom decisions. [Will we walk or ride on the bus to the store?]
4. Using graphs to learn. [Do the corn and bean plants grow at the same rate?] (p. 90)

In one kindergarten, children were discussing their favorite dinosaurs. The teacher cut out a number of different dinosaurs, and each child glued his favorite dinosaur onto a designated row on a chart. The children could see which dinosaur was the class favorite by glancing at the length of the rows. They could also count the dinosaurs. Other records children kept concerned the number of blue- and brown-eyed children in the class, favorite ice cream flavors, and shapes of signs found on the playground. It is important that children always understand the *purpose* of collecting data and keeping a record.

Fractions and decimals

Fractions and decimals should be introduced in the primary grades rather than in nursery schools and kindergartens. Four- and five-year-olds do begin to understand the concept of a half, but other fractional parts appear to be meaningless. Copeland (1972) states, "The idea of requiring the parts to be of the same size, or the same measure, is often not recognized by young children, who want the biggest half" (p. 259). Through cooking experiences children become familiar with a half cup,

31

a half cookie, and a half stick of butter. They can approximate a half glass when pouring juice or milk from a pitcher.

Children should be encouraged to work with a whole and its parts. Putting small balls of clay into a big ball, assembling puzzle pieces, taking construction toys apart, and folding and unfolding paper help children to understand the relationship of the whole to its parts (Charlesworth & Lind, 1990).

Patterns and relationships

Patterning may be defined as "making or discovering auditory, visual, and motor regularities" (Charlesworth & Lind, 1990, p. 203). Patterns can help children to make predictions. Children use something that they have learned to hypothesize the next step in a process. In order to make patterns meaningful to children, teachers should take advantage of the everyday happenings in the classroom. Photographs can be taken each day, for three weeks, of regular events such as arrival at school, group time, outside activities, and dismissal. These pictures can be displayed together and children can be guided in identifying recurring events and patterns. For example, the teacher can point to a picture and ask, "Where else do you see this picture?" "Why do you think the picture is the first one in each row?" "Let's look at the pictures in each row. How are they alike?" "Do these pictures form a pattern?" "Can they be shown on paper?" One kindergarten child drew symbols for each event—a school, a book, a jungle gym, and a house.

Photographs may be taken of routines such as setting the table, putting on socks and shoes, and drawing a picture. To learn more about children's understanding of *sequencing*, teachers can ask themselves, "Is the sequence the same for all children?" "Can they draw the sequence?" "Do they repeat the sequence?" Arrangements of chairs and tables can be observed and photographed. Is there a pattern? If not, can the furniture be rearranged to make a pattern? One pattern of tables might be: round, rectangular, round, rectangular, and so on. Other items that may form patterns are children's clothing, wallpaper, rugs, paintings, and toys. Children can be asked to arrange transportation toys in patterns on a shelf. One kindergarten child's pattern was truck–car–plane, truck–car, truck–car–plane, truck–car.

SUMMARY

Research indicates that children already have many mathematical understandings before they enter preschool. It is the teacher's responsibility to help children expand and reinforce their existing understandings and construct new ones. In guiding children's mathematics experiences, teachers will find it helpful to remember that:

1. Children play an important part in their learning by constructing their own mathematical knowledge.
2. Children learn mathematics best through firsthand, concrete experiences.
3. Children learn mathematics best by manipulating objects and by acting on their environment both mentally and physically.
4. Teachers learn about children's mathematical understandings by observing their actions and listening to their verbalizations.
5. Children learn mathematics from their interactions with other children and adults.
6. Teachers should guide, not direct, children's thinking about mathematics.
7. Concepts in one mathematical content area should be related to one another and to concepts in other content areas.
8. Children learn best when new mathematical experiences relate to what they already know.
9. Children enter preschool and kindergarten with a background of mathematical information.
10. Children are individuals and may not all be at the same developmental level at the same time. Therefore, teachers cannot expect children in a given age group always to respond to mathematical ideas in the same way.
11. Teachers should not underestimate children's mathematical knowledge or their ability to construct mathematical ideas. They must not, however, pressure children into activities for which their mental structures are not ready.

REFERENCES

Althouse, R. (1981). *The young child: Learning with understanding*. New York: Teachers College Press.

Althouse, R. (1988). *Investigating science with young children*. New York: Teachers College Press.

Baker, A., & Baker, J. (1991). *Maths in the mind*. Portsmouth, NH: Heinemann Educational Books.

Baroody, A. J. (1987). *Children's mathematical thinking*. New York: Teachers College Press.

Bjorklund, D. F. (1989). *Children's thinking: Developmental functions and individual differences*. Pacific Grove, CA: Brooks/Cole.

Borke, H. (1975). Piaget's mountains revisited: Changes in the egocentric landscape. *Developmental Psychology, 11*, 240–243.

Bredekamp, S., & Rosegrant, T. (Eds.). (1992). *Reaching potentials: Appropriate curriculum and assessment for young children*, vol. 1. Washington, DC: National Association for the Education of Young Children.

Case, R., Kurland, M., & Goldberg, J. (1982). Operational efficiency and the growth of short-term memory span. *Journal of Experimental Child Psychology, 33,* 386–404.

Charlesworth, R., & Lind, K. K. (1990). *Math and science for young children.* Albany, NY: Delmar.

Copeland, R. (1972). *Mathematics and the elementary teacher* (2nd ed.). Philadelphia: W. B. Saunders.

Copeland, R. (1988). *Piagetian activities.* Eau Claire, WI: Thinking Publications, A Division of McKinley Companies, Inc.

Dixon, G. T., & Chalmers, F. G. (1990). The expressive arts in education. *Young Children, 67*(1), 12–17.

Driscoll, M. (1988, January). Transforming the "underachieving" math curriculum. *ASCD Curriculum Update.*

Dutton, W. H., & Dutton, A. (1991). *Mathematics children use and understand, Preschool through third grade.* Mountain View, CA: Mayfield.

Elkind, D. (1988). Educating the very young: A call for clear thinking. *NEA Today, 6,* 22–27.

Flavell, J. H., Friedrichs, A. G., & Hoyt, J. D. (1970). Developmental changes in memorization process. *Cognitive Psychology, 1,* 324–340.

Fuson, K. C., Richards, J., & Briars, D. J. (1982). The acquisition and elaboration of the number word sequence. In C. J. Brainerd (Ed.), *Children's logical and mathematical cognition: Progress in cognitive development research* (pp. 33–92). New York: Springer-Verlag.

Gallagher, J. M., & Reid, D. K. (1981). *The learning theory of Piaget and Inhelder.* Austin, TX: Wadsworth.

Gelman, R. (1969). Conservation acquisition: A problem of learning to attend to relevant attributes. *Journal of Experimental Child Psychology, 7,* 167–187.

Gelman, R. (1972). Logical capacity of the very young: Number invariance rules. *Child Development, 43,* 75–90.

Gelman, R., & Gallistel, C. R. (1978). *The child's understanding of number.* Cambridge, MA: Harvard University Press.

Ginsburg, H. P. (1980). Children's surprising knowledge of arithmetic. *Arithmetic Teacher, 28*(1), 42–44.

Gothard, H. M., & Russell, S. M. (1990). A tale of two teachers. *Young Children, 66*(4), 214–218.

Ham, D., Perry, J., Corley, R. M., Taylor, J., & Cooper, S. B. (1988). *Continuity of learning for children ages 4, 5, and 6 in South Carolina public schools.* Columbia: South Carolina Department of Education.

Howe, A. C., & Jones, L. (1993). *Engaging children in science.* New York: Macmillan.

Hyde, A. A., & Hyde, P. R. (1991). *Mathwise: Teaching mathematical thinking and problem solving.* Portsmouth, NH: Heinemann.

Inagaki, K. (1992). Piagetian and post-Piagetian conceptions of development and their implications for science education in early childhood. *Early Childhood Research Quarterly, 7,* 115–133.

Jones, L. V. (1988). School achievement trends in mathematics and science, and what can be done to improve them. In E. Z. Rothkopf (Ed.), *Review of research in education, 15, 1988–89* (pp. 307–341). Washington, DC: American Educational Research Association.

Kamii, C. (1982). *Numbers in preschool and kindergarten: Educational impli-*

cations of Piaget's theory. Washington, DC: National Association for the Education of Young Children.

Kamii, C. (1985). *Young children reinvent arithmetic.* New York: Teachers College Press.

Katz, L. G., & Chard, S. C. (1989). *Engaging children's minds: The project approach.* Norwood, NJ: Ablex.

Kreutzer, M. A., Leonard, C., & Flavell, J. H. (1975). An interview study of children's knowledge about memory. *Monographs of the Society for Research in Child Development, 40* (Whole No. 159).

Leeb-Lundberg, K. (1989). Math is more than counting. In J. S. McKee & K. M. Paciorek (Eds.), *Early childhood education 89/90.* Guilford, CT: The Dushkin Publishing Group.

Markman, E. M., & Seibert, J. (1976). Classes and collections: Internal organization and resulting holistic properties. *Cognitive Psychology, 8,* 561–577.

National Association for the Education of Young Children. (1987). *Developmentally appropriate practice in early childhood programs serving children from birth through age 8.* S. Bredekamp (Ed.). Washington, DC: National Association for the Education of Young Children.

National Association for the Education of Young Children & The National Association of Early Childhood Specialists in State Departments of Education. (1991). Guidelines for appropriate curriculum content and assessment in programs serving children ages 3 through 8. *Young Children, 46*(3), 21–38.

National Association of State Boards of Education Task Force on Early Childhood Education. (1988). *Right from the start.* Alexandria, VA: National Association of State Boards of Education.

National Council of Teachers of Mathematics. (1989). *Curriculum and evaluation standards for school mathematics.* Reston, VA: National Council of Teachers of Mathematics.

Piaget, J. (1970). *Science of education and the psychology of the child.* New York: Grossman.

Price, C. G. (1989). Mathematics in early childhood. *Young Children, 44*(4), 53–58.

Pulaski, M. A. (1971). *Understanding Piaget.* New York: Harper & Row.

Resnick, L. B. (1989). On learning research in conversation with Lauren Resnick. *Educational Leadership, 46,* 12–16.

Revelle, L. B., Wellman, H. M., & Karabenick, J. D. (1985). Comprehension monitoring in preschool children. *Child Development, 56,* 654–663.

Schultz, K. A., Colarusso, R. P., & Strawderman, V. W. (1989). *Mathematics for every young child.* Columbus, OH: Merrill.

Seefeldt, C. (1987). The visual arts. In C. Seefeldt (Ed.), *The early childhood curriculum: A review of current research* (pp. 183–210). New York: Teachers College Press.

Shatz, M., & Gelman, R. (1973). The development of communication skills. *Monograph of the Society for Research in Child Development, 38* (Serial No. 152).

Siegler, R. S. (1986). *Children's thinking.* Englewood Cliffs, NJ: Prentice Hall.

Siegler, R. S. (1991). *Children's thinking* (2nd ed.). Englewood Cliffs, NJ: Prentice Hall.

Slavin, R. E. (1988). *Educational psychology*. Englewood Cliffs, NJ: Prentice Hall.

Spodek, B., Saracho, O. N., & Davis, M. D. (1991). *Foundations of early childhood education* (2nd ed.). Englewood Cliffs, NJ: Prentice Hall.

Trafton, P., & Bloom, S. (1990). Understanding and implementing the NCTM curriculum and evaluation standards for school mathematics in grades K–4. *School Science and Mathematics*, *90*(6), 482–486.

Tudge, J., & Caruso, D. (1988). Cooperative problem solving in the classroom: Enhancing young children's cognitive development. *Young Children*, *44*(1), 46–52.

Vukelich, R., & Thornton, S. (1990). Children's understanding of historical time: Implications for instruction. *Childhood Education*, *67*(1), 22–25.

Vygotsky, L. (1962). *Thought and language*. Cambridge, MA: MIT Press.

Wadsworth, B. J. (1984). *Piaget's theory of cognitive and affective development* (3rd ed.). White Plains, NY: Longman.

Whitin, D., Mills, H., & O'Keefe, T. (1990). *Living and learning mathematics*. Portsmouth, NH: Heinemann.

Williams, C. K., & Kamii, C. (1986). How do children learn by handling objects? *Young Children*, *42*(1), 23–26.

PART II

Activities for Investigating Mathematics

The mathematical experiences in Chapters 3–10 are organized around mathematical themes or topics. Katz and Chard (1991) state:

> In some countries, project work is referred to as theme or topic work. Others refer to a project as a unit. Some teachers combine project work with a learning center approach. Although the meanings of these terms vary somewhat, they all emphasize the part of the curriculum that encourages children to apply their emerging skills in informal, open-ended activities that are intended to improve their understandings of the world they live in. (p. xii)

The themes or topics of the following chapters were chosen because children in developmentally appropriate preschools and kindergartens naturally engage in many of the described activities, because the activities are interesting to children, and because they give children the opportunity to construct mathematical concepts at their own level of development. Although each unit focuses on a specific mathematical topic, other mathematical concepts and processes related to the topic are used by children throughout the units. All activities are from the *Standards for Curriculum and Evaluation for School Mathematics*. Only those mathematical understandings considered developmentally appropriate for three-, four-, and five-year-olds have been chosen.

The mathematical processes selected for particular emphasis in the activities throughout the remaining chapters are derived from the *Standards* as follows:

Solving problems (1. *Mathematics as Problem Solving*)
Using mathematical language—talking, dictating, and writing (2. *Mathematics as Communication*)
Thinking about mathematical ideas in order to solve problems (3. *Mathematics as Reasoning*)
Relating mathematical ideas to each other (4. *Mathematical Connections*)

Estimating—area, volume, length, height, and size (5. *Estimation*)

Counting, classifying, using cardinal number, using ordinal number, making comparison, sequencing events, and one-to-one correspondence (6. *Number Sense and Numeration*)

Using spatial relations; using geometrical relations—naming, recognizing, and matching shapes (9. *Geometry and Spatial Sense*)

Measuring, covering surfaces, exploring surfaces, and filling containers (10. *Measurement*)

Keeping records and using charts (11. *Statistics and Probability*)

Making and representing patterns (13. *Patterns and Relationships*)

All of the activities in the chapters have been introduced and expanded with three-, four-, and five-year-old children in five classrooms. Three groups of children were heterogeneous, composed of white, African-American, East Indian, and Asian children primarily from upper-income and middle-income homes. Several low-income and disabled children were also included in each of these three classrooms. Two groups of children were more homogeneous, composed of at-risk white and African-American children.

3 OUR DAY AT SCHOOL
One-to-One Correspondence

In order to count meaningfully, children must be able to assign a number name to each object. Before children learn to enumerate, they must be able to place objects in a one-to-one relationship. "I need two dresses, one for my doll and one for my friend's," "I'm going to put a napkin in front of each chair," "I have a cup and a plate, one for juice and one for salad," and "I only need one piece of drawing paper" are comments that show children's awareness of a one-to-one relationship.

Teachers should not assume, however, that as children interact with materials they will automatically absorb the concept of one-to-one correspondence. Teachers must know how to plan for and guide children through activities that promote an understanding of one-to-one correspondence.

For example, throughout the school day, teachers can focus children's activities on *comparing sets* — a set of children with a set of objects: "Do we have enough paper for everyone at this table? How do you know?" "Do we have enough crayons so that each child can have five? How can we find out?" "Do we have enough balls so that each of you has a ball? How do you know there are enough balls? How can we find out?" Because these questions are not readily solved by counting, they encourage children to use one-to-one correspondence.

Although the focus of this chapter is on one-to-one correspondence, children doing the following activities also use *measurement* (comparing sizes of dolls, doll clothes and dress-up clothes); *classification* (finding doll clothes that "belong" to each doll); *communication* (using mathematical language such as *more than, less than, one, two*, etc.); *problem solving* (finding ways to show *more than, less than*, and *the same as*); and *counting* (counting children, plates, napkins, etc.).

ACTIVITY 1
OUR LOCKERS

Nursery-school and kindergarten classrooms generally have lockers or cubbies in which children keep their belongings. Usually on the first day of school children are either assigned a cubby or choose one. In order to help children identify their cubbies, teachers often place children's photographs or names in their cubbies. Activity 1 is designed to reinforce the concept that each child has a cubby.

Mathematical processes
Using one-to-one correspondence, using mathematical language, and solving problems.

What you need

Cubbies or lockers
Children's extra clothing and/or mats, blankets, and pillows

How you begin
When assigning cubbies at the start of the school year, say to the children, varying your words according to the items parents are asked to send to school,

> You have brought your mats and extra clothing to school. We have cubbies at school to put your things in.
> Do you have a cubby to put your things in?
> Do we have a cubby for every boy and girl?

The children's answers will depend on their age and experience. In one nursery school the children's answers centered around their possessions: "I have a box of clothes to put in my cubby." "I saw the cubbies. I have one for my blanket." "I have my shoes." "See, I have a cubby for my mat." These children were confident that they had cubbies because they had things to put into their cubbies. After discussing the children's answers, say,

> I am going to choose six children to find cubbies to put their _____ in. When you find a cubby, put your _____ in it. The cubby you choose will be your cubby.

Ask the aide or another adult to help the children put their things in the cubbies. When all of the children have placed their belongings in the cubbies, ask them to stand in front of their cubbies. Say to the children,

How do you know which cubby is yours?

Answers to this question will vary. Typical answers from three- and four-year-olds are: "I can sit in my cubby." "I put my blanket in my cubby." "This is my cubby. I can touch it." "Look at my cubby." Five-year-olds' responses are much more sophisticated. Some examples are: "I put my things in this cubby and it's mine." "I am standing in front of my cubby so everyone will know it's mine." "All of us kids have cubbies." "We are all standing in front of our cubbies." One child said, "One, one," as he pointed first to his cubby and then to himself. Other children began to chant, "One, one," as they pointed to themselves and their cubbies.

In one nursery school the children sat in their cubbies while they showed their clothes, pillows, and blankets to each other. Surprised, one child said, "There's a cubby with no one in it." Unknown to the teacher, there was an extra cubby. What to do with the empty cubby? The children wanted to know why there was no child in the cubby. The teacher asked, "Are all the children at school?" Some children said, "Yes," and some said, "No." Then the teacher called the roll and the children learned that everyone was in school. One child then said, "One more children can come to this school," and another child said, "No, let Mrs. Jones have it." It was decided that the teacher could put her books in the cubby.

While the children are standing in front of or sitting in their cubbies, ask, "Will you be able to find your cubby tomorrow?" Most children will say, "Yes, because my things are in it." The next day there will be some children who have difficulty finding their cubbies. Ask the entire group,

What can we do so that each of you can find your cubby?

Use as many of the children's ideas as possible. Suggestions children have given are: "Put our names on them." "I'm going to draw a picture and put it on my cubby." "Put our pictures (photographs) on them." "I want a flower in my cubby." As long as children can identify their cubbies, these need not all be labeled in the same way.

In order to carry out Activity 1, teachers must be able to tolerate some confusion and to *support* rather than *direct* children's thinking. By making mistakes and solving their own problems, children gain confidence in their ability to make and evaluate decisions.

ACTIVITY 2
OUR BODY PARTS

One way to help children think about their body parts is to talk about their eyes, nose, mouth, and ears. They sing action songs about their features and name and touch them as they hear the words of the songs. Finger plays abound that require children to name and touch their features. One way to help children make the one-to-one correspondence between a number name and a body part is to encourage them to *look at* and *touch* body parts as they count them.

Mathematical processes
Using one-to-one correspondence, counting, using mathematical language, and solving problems.

What you need

A stand-up mirror or several hand mirrors

How you begin
Place a stand-up mirror on a table or have several hand mirrors on a nearby table. In small groups say to the children,

> How many eyes do you have?
> How do you know you have two eyes?

Most three- and four-year-olds will say they have two eyes. When asked how they know, some children will point to their eyes and count; others may cover their eyes with their hands and say, "See." One three-year-old held a large magnifying glass in front of his eyes and said, "See, I have two eyes."

Ask the children to look in the horizontal mirror or hand mirrors at their eyes. Ask questions such as,

> How many eyes do you have?
> How many eyes does _____ have?
> Do all the children have two eyes?
> Do I have two eyes?
> Look closely at your eyes. What color are they? Are both eyes the same color?
> Can you find other parts of your body that come in twos?

Children usually say, "ears, legs, and hands." In one nursery school the teacher and children looked in a horizontal mirror and counted their eyes, ears, hands, and legs. They placed their knees on the edge of the table and counted them. Then one three-year-old said, "We have lots of 'ones.'" Surprised, the teacher asked, "What 'ones' do we have?" Sarah answered, "Our nose and chin." Then the children and the teacher looked in the mirror to find body parts that came in "ones." They found their heads, noses, necks, stomachs, and tongues.

After children discuss and count body parts that come in "twos," ask,

Can you find body parts that come in "ones?"
Does each of you have a _____? Everyone has a _____.

Ask children about other body parts. Say,

How many fingers do you have? How many toes?

Allow children to take off their shoes and socks and count their toes. Ask questions such as,

Does everyone have the same number of fingers?
Put your hands against a friend's hand so that your fingers are touching. Are your thumbs touching? Are your little fingers touching? Can you match each finger on _____ hand with one of your fingers? Do you and _____ have the same number of fingers?

One teacher asked three- and four-year-olds how many toes they had. Without exception the three-year-olds replied, "Three," and the four-year-olds answered, "Four."

The teacher took her shoes off and the children counted her red-painted toenails. Then the children took off their shoes and socks and counted their toes. Since the teacher had painted nails, the children wanted their toenails painted. The teacher compromised by helping the children make small paper rings to wear on their toes and fingers. They counted the rings as they put them on their fingers and toes. A few children could not count to five, but they could match a ring to each toe and finger. The children were allowed to go barefooted until the rings fell apart. Some children made replacements; others were satisfied to wear only the finger rings.

Allow children to match body parts to objects such as Unifix cubes, Bristle blocks, colored cubes, and Legos. After placing a Unifix cube on each finger, several kindergarten children placed the cubes in groups of tens and counted 1 ten, 2 tens, 3 tens, etc. One child said, "We have five tens." The teacher helped the children enumerate the objects. Later one child was able to make 10 groups of ten and count 100 objects by tens.

ACTIVITY 3
DRESSING THE DOLLS

Mathematical processes

Counting, using one-to-one correspondence, classifying (belong-to relationships), estimating, using mathematical language, measuring, and solving problems.

What you need

Dolls — four or five multi-ethnic boy and girl dolls of varying heights that are already familiar to the children. No more than two dolls should be the same height. The dolls should be undressed.

Additional dolls — two dolls that are new to the children. One doll should be taller and one shorter than the other dolls.

Doll clothes from the house center — include dresses or pants and shirts, underpants, socks and shoes. These clothes should fit the familiar dolls. Make sure there are enough sets to clothe all the familiar dolls.

Doll clothes that are new to the children — two sets of doll clothes — one set that fits the taller doll and one that fits the shorter doll.

How you begin

Place the familiar dolls and the doll clothes that you have chosen from the house center on a table. Remove any remaining dolls or doll clothes from the center. Leave out the two unfamiliar sets of doll clothes, but not the unfamiliar dolls. Say to the children,

Can you find the clothes that fit the dolls?

Encourage the children to estimate which clothes fit the dolls. Although the children may have dressed the dolls before, they may not realize that some clothes fit more than one doll or that some fit one doll better than another.

After the clothes are chosen, ask questions to focus children's attention on one-to-one correspondence.

Does each doll have clothes?

Does each doll have underpants, dress, pants and shirt, socks, and shoes?

Are the clothes too big? too little? Will they fit another doll?

Point out that there is a set of clothing for each doll and that there are clothes that do not fit any of the dolls. Say to the children,

Do you have more clothes than you need for the dolls?

Will any of the extra clothes fit the dolls?

Are they too big?

Are they too small?

Why don't these clothes fit the dolls?

What size dolls will we need to wear the extra clothes? How many will we need?

Discuss the sizes of the dolls the children will need. Should these be the same size as the dolls they already have? bigger? smaller?

In one nursery school a three-year-old tried to put a too-small pair of long pants on one of the dolls. When they did not fit, he put one pant leg on the doll's arm. Then he took it off and said, "It won't go on. I need a tiny doll."

Later, bring to school the two new dolls that can wear the extra doll clothes. In one nursery classroom, the teacher put the new dolls in the house center without saying anything about them to the children. They found the dolls and dressed them in the extra doll clothes. Then they hurried to their teacher and said, "We found the dolls that fit the clothes."

SNACK TIME

In most nursery schools and kindergartens, children take turns helping teachers set the tables for snack time. All of the children may eat together, or snacks may be staggered. When snacks are staggered, children are free to come to the snack table when they are hungry. Snacks are made available for approximately 30 to 45 minutes. For this activity, it is best to stagger snack time, with small groups of children eating together. However, the activity can also be performed when all of the children eat together. Setting tables for pretend snacks, meals, and parties can also be done in the house center. Teachers can enter children's play in informal and natural ways.

Teachers should guide children's thinking by asking *questions* that encourage the children to place objects in one-to-one correspondence. They should not, however, correct children as they set the tables. Children should be allowed to find and correct their own mistakes to the best of their ability.

Mathematical processes

Using one-to-one correspondence, counting, and solving problems.

What you need

Materials to eat with — include napkins, cups, and plates. Spoons, knives, or forks should be included when needed.

Food for snacks — the foods will vary with each classroom. Include a liquid (which may be water) and a solid so that a cup and a plate are necessary.

How you begin

Remove the chairs from around the snack table. Place plates, cups, and napkins on a counter or a food cart near the snack table. Choose two children to set the table for snack time. If you have a helping chart, tell the helpers it is snack time.

Allow the children to decide how they will set the table. They may put the chairs around the table first and then place a napkin, a plate, and a cup in front of each chair, or they may set the table first and then put a chair in front of each place setting. Encourage the children to set the table with as few directions from you as possible.

In order to set the table, most five-year-olds put the chairs around the table and then count them. Then they count the napkins, plates, and cups and place them one by one in front of each chair. A few five-year-olds will place the napkins, plates, and cups on the table and then put a chair in front of each place setting. Most nursery-school children begin by putting the napkins, plates, and cups haphazardly on the table. Then they put the chairs around the table. When the children sit down for snack, they find that they have more than one napkin, plate, and cup, or none at all. It is obvious to them and the helpers that changes must be made.

Questions teachers can ask to encourage one-to-one correspondence are:

Do you have enough _____ for everyone?
Do you need more _____? How do you know?
Do you have too many _____? How do you know?
Do you have the same amount of _____ as _____?
How can you find out if you have the same amount?

It is possible for children to set a snack table for the entire group. More errors will be made, but these can be corrected by the helpers with the aid of the teacher.

In one nursery school a teacher placed colorful paper plates, cups, and napkins in the house center. Several days later she joined the children and said, "Let's have a party." One child said, "O.K. Let's have a birthday party." Everyone sat down at the table and the teacher asked, "Do we have enough plates for everyone who will be at the party?"

One child counted the people at the table and said, "We have four people." Another child gave each person two plates. The teacher asked, "Why did you give each person two plates?" Susan replied, "That's a plate for lunch and dessert. You need two plates." The teacher asked, "What are we having for lunch?" (The topic had changed from a birthday party to lunch.) Susan replied, "Chinese food. It hasn't cooked yet." She placed a large plate in the middle of the table and said, "This is for more food." Then she put a napkin on each plate and a few in the middle of the table. She said, "In case we need more napkins. We need chopsticks." There were chopsticks in the house center, and Bill gave one to each person. Laura said, "We need two chopsticks." The teacher asked, "What can we do so that we have two chopsticks?" Laura said, "I know." She went to the Manipulative Center and came back with four building sticks to use as chopsticks and gave two to each child. The Chinese food was served and the children ate with chopsticks.

One kindergarten teacher gave the snack helpers seven bananas and several serrated plastic knives. She said, "Give each child half a banana." Mark cut the bananas while Peggy set the table. When the table was set, Mark looked at the banana halves and said, "These aren't the same size." Peggy said, "I know it. It's O.K." She placed a banana piece on each plate. While the children were eating their snack, a few complained, "My banana isn't as big as _____." Peggy's solution was to cut another banana into small pieces and give each child a second piece. This method worked well until all of the banana pieces had been eaten.

When a second group of children came to the snack table, Peggy decided to cut the remaining bananas in half. She asked Mark to help her estimate the halfway mark on each banana. Then she cut them in half. This time there were no complaints from the children. Soon, however, there were no more bananas, even though six children had not had a snack yet. Peggy asked the teacher for more bananas. The teacher asked, "How many do you need?" Peggy said, "I don't know." The teacher gave her five bananas. Instead of cutting all of the bananas, Peggy cut them in half one at a time and distributed the two halves, one to a child, before cutting the next banana. This method was more accurate. Peggy had two bananas left.

When snack helpers make errors, the children eating will usually correct them. They may not be able to offer solutions to the problems, but they will know whether or not each child has the same amount of food, too much, or too little. Teachers can help children solve their problems by asking questions such as,

Does everyone have a _____?
Do you need more _____? What can you do so that each child has one?
Do you have too many _____?
What can you do with the extra _____?

BOYS AND GIRLS AT SCHOOL

During group time, nursery-school and kindergarten teachers often ask children, "How many children are in school today?" "How many boys? How many girls?" Activity 5 encourages children to solve the problem "Are there more girls or boys in school today? How do you know?"

Mathematical processes

Using one-to-one correspondence, counting, communicating, solving problems, and keeping records.

Five-year-old children most often use *counting* to solve this problem, whereas three- and four-year-old children use *one-to-one correspondence.*

What you need

Chart paper
Felt pens
Construction paper

How you begin

During group time, say to the children,

Do we have more girls or more boys in school today?

Guide but do not direct children in finding a solution to this problem. Questions to ask children to help them solve the problem are:

How do you know there are more _____ than _____ in school? How can you find out?
Will it help if the boys stand up? The girls?
Which is more, _____ or _____? How do you know?
How many more _____ than _____ are in school?
Can you think of another way to solve the problem?
How can we remember there are _____ boys, _____ girls, and _____ children in school?

One nursery-school teacher asked a group of three- and four-year-olds, "Do we have more girls or more boys in school today?" A four-year-old replied, "Let me count." He counted 11 boys. Another child said, "No! No! You didn't count yourself." Then Jim said, "O.K., there're twelve boys." Susan said, "I'll count the girls." She counted six girls and then herself. She said, "There are seven girls." The teacher asked, "How do you know there are seven?" Susan replied, "There are two Saras, Laura, Katie, and Leah. And there is Crystal and me. That's seven." The teacher said, "We have twelve boys and seven girls in school. Do we have more girls or more boys in school?" One child said, "Boys. Eleven is more than seven." The teacher asked, "How do you know?" He replied, "Everyone knows that." The teacher accepted this answer and asked, "How many children do we have in school today?" Susan answered, "All of us." Another child said, "I'll count everyone." He counted as far as 14 and stopped. The teacher helped him count the rest of the children. Then she asked, "How can we remember how many boys, girls, and children are here in school?" The children replied, "Write it down."

The teacher made a chart with the names of the days of the week and the words *boys*, *girls*, and *children* under each day. Each day the children used the procedure described above to record the number of children, boys, and girls in school. At the end of the week they discussed the differences in the number of children.

One day, after the children had counted, the teacher asked, "How many more boys than girls are in school today?" Most of the children replied that 11 was more than 7. The teacher repeated the question and said "Think about what I asked you." Then Peter said, "Put a girl beside a boy." This was done and the children counted four more boys than girls.

Next, children can compare the color of their hair and eyes. One nursery-school teacher asked four-year-olds, "Do we have more children with brown hair or more children with blond hair?" Although the children knew three children had black hair and one child had red hair, they included both the black- and the red-haired children with the group of brown-haired children. The following is the dialogue between the teacher and the children.

Teacher:	We have been talking about the color of our hair. Do we have more children with brown hair or blond hair?
Child:	Blond or brown?
Teacher:	Yes, blond or brown hair.
Susan:	I'll count the brown hair. (She counted all the children with brown and black hair, ignoring the black-haired children's protests that they had black hair. Then she counted herself last in spite of the fact that she had red hair.)
Teacher:	What are you counting?
Susan:	Brown hair. Brown hair, stand up. I'm counting. (She counted again, pointing to herself first and then counting—two, three, etc. She again included the black-haired children, since they had stood up when she said, "Brown hair, stand up.")

Susan:	There are thirteen.
Teacher:	Thank you. Would anyone else like to count?
John:	I will. (He counted all of the children standing up. After reaching 10, he no longer assigned a number name to each child, but simply counted by rote to 30.)
Teacher:	How many?
John:	Thirty.
Child:	That's too many.
Teacher:	Can anyone help John?
David:	I can count with my eyes. (He looked at each child, counting slowly and then quickly.) There are thirteen.
Teacher:	Who can count the children with blond hair?
Bill:	I will. Blond hair, stand up. (He counted the blond children, touching each child's head as he counted.) There are seven.
Teacher:	Thank you. We'll count the children again tomorrow.

The teacher did not correct the children who included the black-haired children and red-haired child in the group of brown-haired children. She knew that the children had difficulty dealing with the four groups simultaneously. The next day during group time she said, "Yesterday some of you said you had black hair. Stand up if you have black hair." Three children stood up. "How many children have black hair?"

Child:	Three.
Susan:	I have red hair.
Teacher:	How many children have red hair?
Child:	One.
Teacher:	Stand up if you have brown hair. How many children have brown hair? (This time only the brown-haired children stood up.)
Bill:	I'll count. (He counted nine children with brown hair.)
Teacher:	We have nine children with brown hair. How many children do we have with blond hair?
Bill:	Seven. I counted seven yesterday.
Teacher:	Are there seven here today? Is anyone absent?
Child:	No.
Teacher:	Do we have more children with blond hair or with brown hair?
Child:	Brown hair. Nine is more than seven.
Teacher:	Do we have more children with blond or black hair?
Child:	Blond hair. Seven is more than three.
Teacher:	How can we remember how many children have red, black, blond, and brown hair?
Children:	Write it down.
	Make a chart.

The teacher made a chart with the labels *red hair*, *black hair*, *blond hair*, and *brown hair* written across the top. She provided strips of construction paper corresponding to the children's hair coloring. Each child chose a strip, wrote his or her name on it, and placed it on the chart. The result was a simple chart showing graphically that most children had brown hair.

THOUGHTS ON ONE-TO-ONE CORRESPONDENCE AND CARDINAL NUMBER

Continue throughout the year to encourage children to solve problems through one-to-one correspondence and counting. Whenever possible, record information in the form of *lists*, *charts*, *journals*, and simple *graphs*.

One way to encourage an understanding of "how many" is to ask children to *show* "how many" in a variety of ways. One kindergarten teacher asked the children, "How many ways can you think of to show 'four'?" The children found many ways to express themselves. One child put three strips of plastic clay on a piece of paper and handed the paper and a pair of scissors to the teacher. Another child brought four Unifix cubes. A few children wrote the numeral *4* on the board. Other children brought a box or a manipulative toy with the numeral *4* printed on it. Teachers can encourage three- and four-year-olds to show "three" or "four" and five-year-olds to show "six," "seven," "eight," "nine," and "ten." This is more meaningful than merely counting objects, since children must decide how to define a given set. Children who can show "how many" in more than one way have a better understanding of numbers.

4 OUR ROOM
Classification

Even very young children talk about "belong to" relationships. The two-year-old exclaims, "Mine!" or "My ball!" and the three-year-old says, "This is my truck," and "That's your car." Four- and five-year-old children may say, "The smallest dress belongs to the little doll" or "Put these blocks together. They're red." As they mature, children more accurately determine relationships by closely examining similarities and differences.

After establishing a "belong to" relationship, children begin to sort *like materials*. They may put the red counting bears together, then the blue ones, and finally the yellow ones. *Sorting* is the simplest form of classification. *Multiple classification* requires that children recognize that an object can belong to more than one group. For example, a red bead can belong to the groups "red objects," "wooden objects," and "round objects."

A few five- and six-year-olds understand *class inclusion*, the concept that the whole is greater than its parts. For example, a group of wooden beads includes the subgroups red beads and blue beads, and the subgroups are each smaller than the group of wooden beads. An understanding of class inclusion is necessary for children to understand that four is included in five, three is included in four, two is included in three, and one is included in two.

Teachers can help children to become more discriminating learners by calling attention to similarities and differences between and among objects and allowing children to set up their own criteria for classification. When children group objects according to their own classification systems they must consider a variety of possible characteristics by which to group things.

In the activities in this chapter, children look for likenesses and differences between and among the materials in their room, discuss various uses for the materials, and choose their own criteria for classification. In addition to classification, they explore other areas of mathematics such as *using mathematical language* ("alike," "different," "the same as," and "different from"), *communicating* (discussing why objects belong together), and *solving problems* (choosing criteria for classification). These activities also help children learn more about their classroom and the materials they use in school.

ACTIVITY 1
MATERIALS IN OUR ROOM

Mathematical processes

Classifying, using mathematical language, communicating, and solving problems.

What you need

Materials from the various centers that were not put away. These items will vary from classroom to classroom.

Containers for materials—large baskets, plastic boxes, and/or cardboard boxes.

How you begin

At the beginning of the school year children are becoming familiar with the materials in the various centers. During clean-up time teachers usually encourage children to put materials in the appropriate centers. Usually some materials are left out until a teacher or an aide reminds or encourages the children to put them away.

Instead of having the children return left-out materials to the centers, ask the class to put them in a large container. Bring the container to group time and say to the children,

> There are materials in this container that you played with during center time. Let's look at them together.

Take one object out of the box at a time and say,

> What is this? Which center does the _____ belong in?

Encourage the children to give reasons for their answers. If the children suggest more than one center, ask them why they think the object can belong in each center.

The purpose of Activity 1 is to help the children understand that their teacher has placed in a center items that are alike or belong together. The children may think of reasons for placing objects in other centers.

In the following conversation between a group of four-year-old children and their teacher, several children give answers that are typical of young children who subscribe to *animism*, the belief that inanimate objects have a life of their own.

Teacher: Tell me about this object (a unit block).
Children: It's black.
              It's tan.

54

	Wooden and tan.
Teacher:	It's a wooden block and it does took tan. What center does the block belong in?
Child:	Block center.
Teacher:	Why does it belong in the block center?
Children:	They go there.
	They like to stay there.
	If you don't put it in the block center it will jump out.
Teacher:	How do you use a block?
Children:	Build.
	Play.
Teacher:	Where are the other blocks you use to build?
Children:	In the block center.
	Put it in the block center with the other blocks.
Teacher:	We'll put it in the block center. (Takes apron out of box.) Tell me about this object.
Children:	An apron.
	It's an apron to keep food away.
Teacher:	What center does it belong in?
Child:	House center.
Teacher:	Why do you think it belongs in the house center?
Children:	It loves the house center.
	It gets washed there.
	You can wear it.
	Wear it when you cook.

The teacher and children discussed other items and their physical properties and uses. The "belong to" relationship was stressed.

For several days, continue to encourage the children to think of the centers the materials belong in. Then encourage them to think of the possibility of placing materials in more than one center. Say to the children,

Are there any other centers we could put this object in? Why do you think so?

Encourage the children to give reasons for their answers. Place the objects for several days in each of the centers named by the children.

The following is a conversation between a group of nursery-school children and their teacher, who took a roll of adding-machine tape out of a box.

Teacher:	Where do we keep the tape?
Children:	It belongs in the art center.
	We write on it.

Teacher:	You can use it to write on. What is something else you can do with the tape?
Children:	Color on it.
	Put it in the block center to measure how long the blocks are. (The children had used tape to measure various materials in their room.)
Teacher:	You can use the tape to measure. I'll put a roll of tape in the art center and a roll in the block center.
	(Then the teacher drew a yogurt container from the box.)
Teacher:	What is this? What center does it belong in?
Children:	Food box.
	House center.
	We can put food in it.
	Art center. We can put paint in it.
Teacher:	Food comes in this container. It's a yogurt box. I'll put a few of these containers, two or three, in the house center and a few in the art center. These containers can be used in many ways.

The teacher continued to show the children other materials from the box. She encouraged them to think of different ways to use the materials. Whenever possible, she placed the same kind of material in each of the centers suggested by the children. When there was only one object of a kind, she placed it in one center and then in the other. Later the teacher and children talked about the ways in which they used the object in each center.

Due to its popularity, the teacher and children repeated this activity many times during the year.

PLACING TOYS IN OUR CENTERS

Mathematical processes

Classifying, using mathematical language, solving problems, and keeping records.

What you need

Three or four new toys, or classroom toys that have *not* been introduced to the children. Choose toys that have many possibilities for classification. For example, one teacher chose a set of plastic keys, magnetic people, a bucket, and Post-it notes. Other toys that have many possibilities are stuffed animals, plastic containers, notepads, and water pumps.

A large box or basket

How you begin

Place the toys in a large box and bring it to group time. Say to the children,

> There are toys in this box that you haven't played with in our room. I want you to help me decide which center they belong in.

Take a toy out and say,

> Let's talk about this toy. What do you think it is?

Questions that teachers can ask to help children think about the properties of the objects, their similarities to other objects, and their uses are:

> What is the toy made of?
> Is it made of more than one material?
> Does it have more than one part?
> How can it be used?
> What center do you think it belongs in?
> How is this toy like the other toys in the center?
> Why do you think so?
> Could it be placed in more than one center?
> How could it be used?
> How is it like the toys in this center?
> Which of the centers do you want to put it in first? second? third?

Most groups of children will come to an agreement about the centers. If not, they can vote on which center to put the toy in first and how long to keep it in a center. Ask the children,

How long should the toy be in a center?

Answers to this question will vary. Children may say, "Two days," "Three days," or "A week." Ask the children,

How will we know when the toy has been in a center for that long?

Some of the answers given by nursery-school and kindergarten children to this question are: "Mark it on the calendar," "Make a mark on paper every day," "Make a chart and check off each day," and "Count." Help the children formulate a plan for recording the length of time the toy is in a center. In one kindergarten the children marked off the required number of days on the class calendar.

The following dialogue between a group of kindergarten children and their teacher began when the teacher showed the children a new toy, a set of large plastic keys. Only one child in the group realized it was a toy designed for a baby.

Teacher:	What is this toy?
Children:	Plastic keys.
	Colored keys.
	Big keys to hold.
	For a baby (said so softly that the children and teacher didn't hear her).
Teacher:	These are plastic keys. How could they be used?
Children:	Throw them out the window. We'll find them and open a car in the parking lot.
	Those aren't real keys.
	They won't open a car and you'll lose them.
Child:	I was just kidding.
Teacher:	Can you think of another way to use them?
Children:	Give them to the mommy to give to the baby. (The recorder was sitting close to the child and heard what she said. The teacher did not hear her.)
	Use them to start a pretend car.
	Trace around them.
	Shake them.
Teacher:	Which center do they belong to?
Children:	Block center to crank up a car.
	Manipulative center to shake and open car doors. (The cars were made from construction toys.)
	House center to open the door.
	House center for the baby to play with. (Said very softly, but this time the teacher noticed that Karen was trying to tell her something.)
Teacher:	Karen, tell us again. We couldn't hear you. (Karen repeated what she said.)

Teacher:	The babies could play with the keys in the house center. Why do you think the babies would like this toy?
Child:	Because it's a baby toy.
Teacher:	Why do you think it's a baby toy?
Child:	The keys are big so a baby can't swallow them. It's a baby toy.
Teacher:	You're right. It is a toy for a real baby. It can be used in many ways.

The teacher continued to discuss with the children the toy, its properties, its uses, and the appropriate centers to place it in:

Teacher:	Where do you want to put the toy first? The house center? the block center? the art center? or the manipulative center?
Child:	The house center. We need a key to open the door. A key for the front door and a key for the back.
Teacher:	There are three keys.
Child:	I know! A key for the car.
Teacher:	First, you want to put the keys in the house center. Where do you want to put them second?

It was decided to put the keys second in the block center, third in the art center, and fourth in the manipulative center. The children decided the keys would be kept in a center for seven days, or one week. Each day one of the children drew a picture of something significant that happened during the school day. These pictures were placed on the wall in sequence to form a picture calendar. On the first day of the school week the keys were placed in the house center. A child drew a picture of the keys in the center and put an X on the picture. The picture was added to the calendar and for six more days an X-marked picture was placed on the calendar. At the end of seven days the keys were moved to another center.

During the year, whenever a new toy is introduced, allow the children to help decide which center or centers to put it in.

ACTIVITY 3
MAKING COLLAGES

Mathematical processes

Using mathematical language, classifying, and solving problems.

What you need

Materials that vary in shape, texture, and/or color but are small enough to be glued onto a 9″ × 12″ sheet of paper, such as pom-poms (which should differ in size and color), assorted buttons, cut straws, colored macaroni (two or three different colors), cotton balls, coffee stirrers, tongue depressors, popsicle sticks, stickers of various shapes and colors, etc.

Containers — large ones to hold collage materials for the class and small ones (meat trays, box lids, small boxes, etc.) for the children's individual materials.

Scissors

Glue

Construction paper (9″ × 12″)

How you begin

Choose five or six different materials and put them in separate containers. Place the containers near the table where the children are going to work. On the children's table(s) place glue, scissors, and a selection of colored construction paper.

Addressing small groups of not more than six children, say,

I have materials for you to make collages. Let's look at them together.

Talk about the materials in each of the boxes — their shapes, sizes, colors, and textures. Most of the materials should be familiar to the children. If colored macaroni are used the children can dye them several days in advance. Say to the children,

Find a small container to hold your materials. Take as many materials from the large containers as you think you will need to make a collage.

Observe the children as they gather their materials. Ask yourself: Were there children who chose samples of each various material? Were there children who chose a limited variety of materials? As the children come to the table to work and select construction paper, say to them,

Put the materials that are alike in some way together. You may put them on the table in front of you.

While the children classify materials, ask questions such as,

How are the _____ and _____ alike?
How are they different from the _____?
Can you think of other ways they are alike?
Could the _____ belong in more than one group? Why do you think so?

Ask yourself: Did the children put objects of the same material together? Did they group together nonidentical but similar materials?

In one nursery school the teacher put out cotton balls, crushed eggshells, buttons, pom-poms, red and blue macaroni, cut straws, and shapes cut from construction paper. One child in the class of three- and four-year-olds made the following groupings:

Cotton balls
Large pom-poms
Small pom-poms
Straws
Red macaroni
Blue macaroni

The child's reason for the grouping: "They are all alike. I picked different things because I wanted different things in my picture." Another child made the following groupings:

Cotton balls and large pom-poms
Buttons
Large and small macaroni
Straws

The reason given for the grouping: "I put the things that are alike together. They are mostly round. I chose different things because my mother doesn't like all of one thing." Here is a third set of groupings:

Triangular pieces of paper and triangular pieces of eggshell
Pom-poms
Red macaroni
Blue macaroni

The reason for the grouping: "I put the pom-poms together. Some are big and some are little. I put triangles together — paper triangles and these triangle eggshells. I like triangles; I put red macaroni in one pile and blue in one pile. I'm going to make a pretty picture."

Most nursery-school children sorted the materials and put them in separate groups. A few grouped objects that were similar, but not exactly alike — for example, the triangular pieces of eggshells and paper, and the cotton balls and large pom-poms.

In one kindergarten the teacher put out the same materials as the ones in the examples above. One of the <u>five-year-olds</u> made the following groupings:

Straws and macaroni
Cotton balls and pom-poms
Eggshells

The reason given for the grouping: "The straws and macaroni are long. The cotton balls and pom-poms feel soft. The shells aren't like anything else." Another child's groupings were:

Eggshells and macaroni
Buttons
Straws

The reason: "You can cook macaroni and eggs. Buttons are round. Straws are long."

The groupings of the older children were more sophisticated than those of the younger children. Some of the kindergarten children were able to use *multiple classification*: When asked to regroup the materials, they placed items in different groupings.

Throughout the year, encourage children to group all kinds of materials and to give reasons for their groupings.

ACTIVITY 4
PLANNING OUR CENTERS

Mathematical processes

Using mathematical language, classifying, solving problems, and keeping records.

What you need

Materials in the room
Children's name cards
Box for children's name cards

How you begin

Have the children's name cards available to draw names. During group time say to the children,

> I want you to think of the activities you would like to have in the centers tomorrow. We'll take turns and four of you can help me set up the centers. Everyone will have a turn.

Talk with the children about each center and what they would like to do there. If the children choose two or more activities that cannot be supervised adequately, explain why the activities cannot be done on the same day. Include them the next day or later in the week. Children may suggest activities that are impossible to carry out. One child suggested roasting hot dogs in the house center. Instead, during snack time the children boiled hot dogs in the kitchen.

The following is the dialogue between a nursery-school teacher and the children:

Teacher: What would you like to do in the house center?
Children: Play telephone.
Call each other on the telephone.
Change the doll's clothes.
Cook dinner.
Teacher: I'll write all of your suggestions on a notepad. What would you like to do in the library center?
Children: Look at books.
Look at the book about the hungry caterpillar.
Teacher: I wrote your suggestions on the notepad. What would you like to do in the block center?
Child: Build tall houses.
Teacher: What would you like to do in the manipulative center?

Children:	Play with bristle blocks.
	Build rockets.
Teacher:	What would you like to do in the art center?
Children:	Finger painting.
	Draw pictures.
Teacher:	What would you like to do in the science center?
Children:	Play with magnets.
	Play in the sand. There is sand in the sand table for us to use.
Teacher:	I wrote your suggestions on my notepad. I'll read them to you.

The teacher read the list and then drew four names from among the name cards. She read the names and said, "These children can help today. Tomorrow I'll draw four more names from the box. Every day I'll draw four names until every boy and girl has had a turn."

Ask the four helpers to assist you in setting up the centers for the next day. If necessary, have the aide or a volunteer supervise the rest of the children for the remainder of the group time. In one preschool classroom it took approximately 20 minutes to set up the centers.

Read the list to the children as you and they move from center to center. Stress with them the relationships among the materials found in a center. The art center is given as an example. Similar questions can be asked about any center:

What do the children want to do tomorrow in this center?
What do they need for the center?
Is everything here that they need?
What belongs with the drawing paper?
If the children want to draw, will they need any other materials?
How are all of the materials you chose for drawing pictures alike?
Can all of them be used to draw?
Can any other materials be used that you haven't put out?
How are they like the materials you already chose?

Not all of the above questions will be necessary. In some cases children will put out a few materials and completely ignore others. For example, one kindergarten group put out crayons but, until questioned by the teacher, left out felt-tip pens and pencils.

In the example of the nursery school given above, the four helpers included and/or arranged the following materials:

House center
Sorted doll clothes into big and little.
Put pots and pans together below the sink.
Placed notepads and pencils near the phones.

Library center
Made sure *The Hungry Caterpillar* was on the shelf.

Block center
Moved Crystal Climbers from the manipulative center to the block center—"to build tall buildings."

Found several small empty boxes—"to build with. They won't hurt you if they fall."

Art center
Chose finger-painting paper.

Chose yellow and blue finger paint "to make green."

Filled spray bottles with water "to wet paper."

Checked to make sure there was drawing paper, crayons, felt pens, and pencils.

Manipulative center
Put out bristle blocks.

Put out Legos "to build rockets."

Science center
Put out magnets.

Put out a few more sand toys.

Continue to choose helpers until all of the children have had a turn. While involved with these activities teachers found that it was best to give every child a turn over a period of five to seven days. Later they repeated the activity once a week or every two weeks. This activity was very popular with the children, who made remarks such as "I know what we can do next week in the _____ Center" and "I found something to put in the _____ Center."

THOUGHTS ON CLASSIFICATION

It is important for teachers to help children learn the *physical properties* of objects and the *relationships* between and among objects. When children know the characteristics and functions of objects, they are better able to classify objects according to their similarities. In learning how objects are similar, children also learn how they are different.

5 OURSELVES
Linear Measurement

Young children like to talk and learn about themselves. They boast that they are "big" and "strong." They say that they are "almost three," or "three-and-a-half" rather than "three" years old. When one child celebrated her third birthday and her teacher commented, "You are a big girl now," Julie replied, "No, now I'm a child." She was no longer a baby or a toddler.

Children often show how tall they are by holding their hand just above their heads and saying, "I'm this tall." They may stand beside an object or their teacher and say, "I'm almost as tall as this," or "I come to 'here' on you."

The activities in this chapter encourage children to match and compare objects to determine the "biggest" and the "smallest." The terms *taller*, *shorter*, and *longer* are used by the teacher after children have matched many objects and made verbal comparisons. Later children are encouraged to *show*, *measure*, and *talk about* how tall they are "from top to bottom." Since most young children do not conserve length, nonstandard units of measurement are used. Children measure body parts and objects with single units of measurement such as adding-machine paper, string, or yarn. They also measure by aligning units, such as coffee stirrers, along the objects to be measured. They are encouraged to count the number of units it takes to measure an object. Although the activities focus on *measurement*, children have opportunities to *estimate* (match and compare objects); *communicate* (talk about body parts and objects); *use spatial relations* (put together paper strips representing the body); *enumerate* (count body parts); *solve problems* (make something for the room); and *make mathematical connections* (use mathematical processes to reason and solve problems).

The following activities should be carried out in groups of no more than four nursery-school or six kindergarten children. Teachers who helped to develop the activities found that they could help individual children best during Learning Center Time, when the aide could supervise the other activities.

Some children were involved in these activities for approximately five weeks. The length of time depended on the ages of the children and their interest in the activities. Children should not be hurried through the activities, since they need time to solve problems to their satisfaction. It is not necessary for every child to be involved in all of the activities or in an activity every day.

ACTIVITY 1
MATCHING OBJECTS

Mathematical processes

Matching, making comparisons, estimating, using mathematical language, using spatial relations, and measuring.

What you need

Objects found in the room

How you begin

Ask a small group of children,

Can you find something in the room that is "as tall as you are tall"?

Encourage the children to discover many objects that are "as tall as they are tall." Move around the room with the children and talk with them about the objects they find. Ask the children,

What have you found that is as tall as you are tall? How do you know?
Can you find something that is taller than you are tall?

One three-year-old said, "The board is bigger than me. It's high," and another child, looking in a stand-up mirror, said, "I see the top of the mirror over me." Some comments made by five-year-olds were, "Look, the shelf is only a little taller than me," "I'm as tall as the top of the chalkboard," and "I'm this much [spreading thumb and forefinger apart] taller than the shelf." If children have not already found something in the room that is shorter than they are tall, ask them,

Can you find something that is not as tall as you are?

In one nursery school a four-year-old shouted, "Look, I'm bigger than everything!" A three-year-old girl stood in front of a wall chart and said, "I'm tall." The teacher asked, "Is the chart taller than you are?" Laurie replied, "I don't know," and tried to reach the top of the chart with her hands. The teacher placed a stand-up mirror in front of her. Laurie looked in the mirror and said, "The chart's bigger than me." Three- and four-year-olds may make comparisons by using the words "bigger" and "smaller" rather than "taller" and "shorter." This is typical of their age and should be accepted by the teacher. After children become familiar with the terms *taller* and *shorter*, they will begin to use them appropriately.

After children have compared their heights with objects, ask them to match and compare objects in the room. Say to them,

> Can you find objects in the room that are as tall as the _____ (table, building block, bookshelf, book)?

In one preschool classroom, comments made by the children were, "The puzzle is shorter than the book," "This book is littler than this block," "Look, the parakeet's cage is taller than the gerbil's," and "The paint cups are all the same [height]."

Teachers should encourage children to match and compare as many objects as possible by placing them on top of or beside each other. The terms *taller* and *shorter* should be used when objects are perpendicular to the floor, and *longer* and *shorter* when they are parallel to the floor.

If children become interested in comparing their heights, teachers can accept their comments matter-of-factly, without calling attention to the "tallest" and "shortest" children in the class. Teachers should never compare children's heights out loud or place children in a row from shortest to tallest.

Children can learn to *compare visually* the length of objects. Ask children to look at objects. Then say,

> Do you think the (bulletin board, bookcase, etc.) is taller than the (toy shelf, table, etc.)? How can you be sure?

Visual comparison of objects is more difficult for three-year-olds than for four- and five-year-olds. One three-year-old said, "The chair looks big," whereas a five-year-old said, "I know I'm taller than the chair." The teacher asked the five-year-old, "How do you know?" The child said, "I can tell by looking." Then she stood beside the chair and said, "See, I'm taller."

Encourage children to check their observations by placing one object beside or on top of another object. They may spend several days matching objects.

ACTIVITY 2
MEASURING OURSELVES

Mathematical processes

Measuring, solving problems, and using mathematical language.

What you need

Several rolls of adding-machine paper
Scissors
Containers to hold paper strips

How you begin

Unroll the adding-machine paper at least 2 feet and ask a small group of children,

How can you use the paper strip to show how tall you are?

Children will react differently to the question, depending on their age and experience. One four-year-old immediately lay on the floor and said, "Do me" ("Measure me"). The teacher responded by unrolling the paper beside the child's body. When she reached his head, she stopped, stood up, and held the paper to show him how long he was "from top to bottom." She asked, "Is this paper as long as you are tall?" John stood up and said, "Yes, put the paper at the bottom of my shoes. It will reach my head."

Children will devise different ways to measure their heights with the rolls of paper. Allow them to make their own decisions and their own mistakes. One four-year-old tried to measure himself as he lay on the floor. He put the end of the paper under the heel of his shoe and unrolled the paper along his body. He repeated the same procedure several times before asking for help in cutting the paper. Another child taped the paper to the toe of his shoe and, standing up, unrolled it against his body. When the paper reached his head, he said to the teacher, "Cut the paper. I can't." Children may choose to work in pairs, taking turns measuring each other. They will need the teacher's help in holding and cutting or tearing the paper. After children have used the paper to measure body parts, label each strip with the child's name and body part.

Encourage children to check their measurements against their paper strips. Ask questions such as,

Is the strip of paper "as tall as you are tall"?
How do you know?
Show me.

Some children may want to use the adding-machine paper to measure and compare objects in the room. Encourage these activities and ask questions about the objects:

Is the pegboard longer than the puzzle?
How much longer is it?
How do you know?

Help children to understand that the measurements "long" and "tall" may mean the same thing. Remember to refer to objects that are parallel to the floor as "long" and those that are perpendicular as "tall." Begin to use the terms *measure* and *height* with the children. Comments such as "Use the paper to measure your height" and "The paper shows your height or how tall you are" help children to learn these terms.

MEASURING BODY PARTS

Mathematical processes

Solving problems and making comparisons.

What you need

Several rolls of adding-machine paper

How you begin

Children may already have begun measuring other parts of their bodies on their own. If not, ask small groups of children,

How would you use the paper strip to measure your arm?

Encourage the children to measure their arms and any other parts of their bodies they want to measure. Children who work in pairs may still need help in cutting or tearing the paper. Four- and five-year-old children are usually more interested in these activities than are three-year-olds. There are, however, some younger children who will continue to measure until they have measured most of their body parts. A few five-year-olds will include fingers and toes as well as hands and feet. One kindergarten child took off her shoes and socks and carefully measured each toe. In the process, the paper strips for the right and left feet got mixed up. When Susan put the papers together to represent her toes, she said, "They [paper strips] look funny." The teacher asked, "Are your toes the same length? Look at your toes." Susan took off her shoes and socks and examined her toes. Then she measured each toe with a paper strip. If a strip didn't match, she tried another strip. She continued until each strip matched a toe.

When children have measured several parts of their bodies, encourage them to compare the paper strips by asking,

Are your arms the same length? Your legs?
Is your arm longer than your hand? leg?
Is your body longer than your legs?
How do you know?

Children may measure the length or the circumference of their heads. Either method should be accepted. Label the strips of paper representing body parts and place them in envelopes or boxes. Later the children can arrange the strips to represent their bodies.

This activity may continue for several weeks. Younger children sometimes lose interest in the activity but return to it later. Not all children will measure every body part. Typically, they will measure their head, arms, legs, and height. A few will measure their trunks, hands, fingers, feet, and toes.

PUTTING BODY PARTS TOGETHER

Mathematical processes

Using spatial relations, using cardinal number, and solving problems.

What you need

Envelopes or boxes containing paper strips representing children's body parts

Large pieces of mural paper, preferably colored

Stand-up mirror

How you begin

Work with no more than two or three children at a time. Give the children their envelopes or boxes containing the paper strips representing their body parts. Say to them,

> Take out the paper strips. Find the paper strip that is as tall as you are tall.

Help the children tape or paste the paper strips showing their height on the mural paper. Place one end of the strip even with the bottom edge of the paper. Put the stand-up mirror near the children.

After the paper strips are fastened to the mural paper, ask the children to look at the remaining strips of paper. Help them to find the strips that represent their arms by asking,

> How many arms do you have?
> Find the strips of paper that show how long your arms are.
> Where would you put them on the strip of paper that shows how tall you are?
> Look in the mirror. Where are your arms?

Continue to encourage the children to examine their paper strips. Say to them,

> Look at your other paper strips. Can you tell which part of your body each one measures?
> Put the paper strips on the mural paper where you think they belong. You may want to look in the mirror.

Allow the children to make mistakes without correcting them. One three-year-old confused his legs with his arms. His teacher did not correct him, but allowed him to finish attaching all his body parts to the paper. When George looked at his paper, he said, "It doesn't look right." The teacher said, "Let's look at your arms and legs. Where did you put your arms? your legs?" He said, "My arms are long. My legs are short. That's not me." The teacher helped him to reverse his legs and arms.

Most children realize immediately when their "picture" does not look right. One five-year-old placed her head measurement above her body measurement. For several days she did not notice that this arrangement made her taller. One day she looked at the "picture" of her taped on the wall. She said loudly, "I'm not that tall." Her teacher said, "What do you think happened?" Lindsey stood beside the paper and said, "I don't know, but it's taller than me." Her teacher pointed to the paper strip representing Lindsey's height and asked, "What part of you does this measure?" She said, "Me, from head to toe." Before the teacher could ask another question, Lindsey said, "I put my head above my body. My head was already there."

A few children may not have paper strips for all of their body parts. If they want to, allow them to put together the measurements that they have made. One four-year-old had paper strips showing his height, an arm, and a leg. When he had taped the paper strips on the mural paper, he laughed and said, "That's me. I'm falling." The teacher asked, "What can you do about it?" He said, "Make another leg and arm." When they see the paper strips taped on mural paper, children usually want to complete their measurements.

Some children may want to tear off the paper showing their height at the place where their trunk ends. They can extend the paper strips representing their legs from the paper trunk.

Children should be encouraged to work together whenever possible. They enjoy helping each other and become almost as excited over another child's "picture" as over their own.

A few children may prefer to take their paper strips home. One three-year-old became very attached to his measurements. He held up a strip of paper and said, "This is my leg." Then he placed the strip along his leg to show that he was correct. He continued until he had matched each strip with a body part. Later he said, "I want to take my strips home and show my mama."

When the children have discussed and admired their "pictures," allow them to take them home.

ACTIVITY 5
OTHER WAYS OF MEASURING

Mathematical processes

Measuring, solving problems, using cardinal number, using mathematical language, estimating, and keeping records.

What you need

Balls of string
Yarn
Adding-machine paper
Some of the following (at least 50 to 100 of each kind): Coffee stirrers, popsicle sticks, straws, dowels (all the same length), unsharpened pencils, and tongue depressors

How you begin

Place several rolls of adding-machine paper, yarn, and string on a shelf. Say to the children,

> You may use the paper, yarn, and string to measure objects in the room.
> I will help you if you need me.

One group of five-year-old children measured the width of their room. The teacher held a ball of string while the children unwound it as they walked across the room. They decided to measure the length of the room in the same way. Then they compared the length of the strings and decided that the room was longer "up and down" and shorter "across." The teacher told them that the "length" of the room was longer than the "width" of the room. When appropriate, teachers should use the terms *length* and *width* with children.

Three- and four-year-olds enjoyed measuring small objects such as puzzles, blocks, boxes, and pegboards. One four-year-old boy used a piece of string to measure the four sides of a puzzle. He cut the string, held it up, and said, "This is how long the puzzle is." The teacher said, "Show me what you did." The child showed her how he had measured around the puzzle with the string. The teacher said, "The string shows how far it is around the puzzle."

Teachers should not use the word *perimeter* with young children. They should, however, make it clear to the children that they are measuring the distance around an object.

After children have experimented with a single unit of measurement, add other objects to the string, yarn, and paper. Coffee stirrers, straws, dowels, and popsicle sticks are easily manipulated by children. Ask a small group of children,

Do you know the names of these objects?

Talk about the different ways the objects are used. Stirrers, for example, are used to stir coffee, dowels to hold pieces of wood together, and popsicle sticks to hold ice cream.

After talking about the various objects, say,

How could you use the _____ to measure your hand?

Allow the children to measure their hands or any other parts of their bodies with the available objects. Some children will use more than one kind of object to measure. One five-year-old said, "My hand is a coffee stirrer and almost one dowel long." Other comments made by the children were: "My hand is two dowels long." "I'm going to cut the straw. It's too long." "My hand is almost a popsicle stick long." "My hand is longer than a stirrer."

If children have not already begun measuring more than one part of their bodies with the objects, you can say,

How many dowels do you think it will take to measure your arm? How many straws? Will it take more straws or more dowels?

How many coffee stirrers do you think it will take to measure your foot? Does it take more stirrers or more popsicle sticks?

How many straws will it take to measure your foot? What can you do if the straw is too long?

Will it take more straws or more pencils to measure your leg? How many more?

In one classroom a child wanted to record his findings. He said to the teacher, "Write what I tell you on paper. I'll write my name." The teacher said, "What shall I write?" The child replied, "My leg is four straws long." Other children, too, become interested in keeping a record of their measurements. One five-year-old made a book of her measurements. She named it "I."

Teachers can encourage record keeping by asking children,

How can you remember how many _____ it took to measure your height? hand? arm? leg?

Most children will ask their teachers to write what they tell them about their measurements. A few children may want to paste the objects used to measure their body parts on large sheets of paper. Encourage children to record as much information as possible. Younger three-year-olds may not be interested in recording any information, but will readily talk to the teacher about what they are doing.

Children may prefer to measure objects rather than body parts. The teacher can encourage children to use *estimation* by asking questions such as,

How many _____ do you think it will take to measure the length of the table?

How many _____ will it take to measure the book? Will you need more _____ or more _____ to measure the _____? How do you know?

Why do you think it took more _____ than _____ to measure the _____?

One group of five-year-olds learned about dinosaurs and wanted to show the length of a brontosaurus. Since the information they found was given in feet, a paper strip was used to measure the length of a ruler. Then the teacher helped them cut many strips of paper 1 foot long. The children taped the strips end to end on the hall carpet until they had taped the correct number of strips. This was a time-consuming group project. When one child got tired, another child would take his or her place. The children's efforts were rewarded by the exclamations of the first graders. Comments made were: "I didn't know a dinosaur was that long." "That dinosaur was as tall as a building." "I'm going to walk beside the paper. I'll walk a long way." "Boy, were dinosaurs big."

Children should continue measurement activities as long as they are interested. The tools for measurement should be available to them every day. Many children will return again and again to measure an object of interest.

OUR SHAPES IN THE CLASSROOM
Shapes

Everything has a shape, and children learn very early to recognize objects by their shape. Soon after birth they know the difference between their mother's face and other adult faces. By interacting with their environment they learn to recognize objects by their shapes. They learn the differences between teddy bears and rabbits, plates and cups, chairs and tables, and triangles and squares. Although children may not know the names of common geometrical shapes, they can pick out shapes that look alike. Names of geometrical shapes are learned after children have had many experiences with them in their concrete form. Building with blocks, putting construction toys together, playing in boxes, and setting the table for snack time give children the opportunity to interact with these shapes in a functional way.

The purpose of the following activities is to help children recognize that everything has a shape, to identify objects by their shapes, and to name a few shapes such as *circles*, *rectangles*, *squares*, and *triangles*.

ACTIVITY 1
EVERYTHING HAS A SHAPE

Mathematical processes

Using spatial relations, making comparisons, and using mathematical language.

What you need

Objects in the room

How you begin

With small groups of 6 to 10 children, talk about objects that look alike. Show the children two animals that are otherwise alike but differ in size—for example, a small and large giraffe, a small and large elephant, and a small and large horse. Say to the children,

> What is the name of these animals?
> How are they alike?
> How are they different?
> Are there any other animals like these in the room?

Talk with the children about the characteristics of the animals. Ask them,

> How do we know they are the same animal?
> How are they different?
> Are they the same size?
> Are they made of the same material?

Compare other objects in the room and use the words "alike" and "different." After the children have talked about objects that are alike and different, say,

> Find two objects in the room that are alike in some way and bring them to the group.

Give the children the opportunity to explain why they chose their objects.

The following is the dialogue between a teacher and a group of three- and four-year-old children:

Teacher:	Children, yesterday you looked at your feet. Were they alike?
Child:	Yes, looked alike.
Teacher:	When you made footprints in the paint with your feet, did your footprints look alike?
Children:	Yes.

	Mine looked the same.
	I had five toes here and here (pointing to feet).
Teacher:	Did all of your footprints look alike?
Children:	No.
	Yes, they are all feet.
	Some were big; some little.
Teacher:	Yes, they look alike because they were all footprints.
	Look around the room and find two things that look alike and bring them to the circle.

The children brought their objects to the group. Among the pairs of objects chosen were two small cars, a magnifying glass and a bowl, a triangular puzzle piece and a block, a bead and a ball, two square blocks, a book and a piece of paper, and two pieces of play dough.

Teacher:	John, tell us how your objects are alike.
Child:	They are both round. (Looks at the bowl, then moves his fingers around the magnifying glass.)
Teacher:	Yes, they have a round shape. Are all bowls round?
Children:	Yes.
	No, there are round pans.
Teacher:	Are pans round?
Child:	No, flat.
Teacher:	What shape is the bottom of most pans?
Child:	Rectangle.
Teacher:	Susan, get three pans from the housekeeping center and let's look at them together.
Children:	The pans are flat.
	The pans' bottoms are rectangles.
Teacher:	Yes, these pans are shaped like rectangles. Jan, show us your objects.
Child:	This is a bead and ball. They are both round.
Teacher:	Yes, they are both round. Jill, show us your objects.
Child:	They are both cars.
Teacher:	Are they the same size?
Child:	No, but they are cars. They look like cars.
Teacher:	Yes, they are car-shaped.

The conversation continued until the children had described their objects.

Encourage the children to talk about the attributes of their objects including shape. Refer to objects as shaped like cars and car-shaped. Ask questions such as,

Why do you think both objects are _____-shaped?
Do they both have _____?
Does this make them _____-shaped?
Does everything have a shape?
Do you have a shape?
Does everyone have a shape?
What is alike about our shapes?

Encourage the children to talk about what makes them people-shaped. You may want to provide a stand-up mirror so they can look at themselves. Ask questions and make comments such as,

Do you have a head? Does everyone have a head? Does everyone have legs? arms? a body?
We are shaped like people. We are people-shaped.

Continue to encourage the children to look for similar-looking objects during learning center time. Talk with them about objects that are the same shape but may differ in size, color, etc. Remind them that they can recognize these objects by their *shape*.

Have a separate area of the room to which the children can bring their objects. Provide paper, pencils, and crayons so that the children can draw around their objects. Ask the children,

Look at the outlines of your objects. Do they look alike? Are they the same shape?

ACTIVITY 2
OBJECTS CAN BE RECOGNIZED BY THEIR SHAPES

Mathematical processes

Using geometrical relations, making comparisons, using mathematical language, and solving problems.

What you need

Objects found in the room that have the same and different shapes — blocks, cars, animals, puzzle pieces, construction toys, etc. Some objects should be the same shape and size; others should be the same shape but different sizes.
White bed sheet
Overhead projector or spotlight
Tray for objects
Table for objects
Cloth
A few unfamiliar objects
Drawing paper
Crayons
Felt-tip pens

How you begin

The purpose of the activity is to show children that objects can be *identified by shape alone.* A silhouette of an object can be made by holding the object behind a sheet and shining a bright light from behind the object, through the sheet.

Find a suitable place in the classroom to hang a sheet. In one classroom some of the teachers tied a string across the room and draped the sheet over it. You should test a variety of two- and three-dimensional objects with the light to make sure their silhouettes are sharp and distinct.

In small groups of 6 to 10, ask the children to sit in front of the sheet. Show the children how, when the light is moved behind an object, its shadow or silhouette can be seen on the sheet. Show them a tray and say,

> I covered an object on this tray with a cloth. I'm going to hold the object behind the sheet. Can you tell me what it is?

Choose an easily identified object such as a toy rabbit, a plate, or a block. When the children have identified a few objects, introduce three objects in succession that have the same shape, such as three toy rabbits, cars, or blocks. Ask the children to identify each object. Then place all of the objects on a table placed in front of the group. Say to the children,

> You can't see the objects. How do you know what they are? How are they alike?

The children may know the names of the objects as well as their shapes. One child said, "They are all trees and triangles."

Encourage the children to name the *geometrical shapes* of the objects they see. Most five-year-olds are familiar with triangles, squares, rectangles, and circles; four-year-olds with triangles and circles; and three-year-olds with circles. Squares and rectangles look very much alike to young children. After hearing the shapes' names associated with objects, they begin to see the differences between the shapes. Teachers can comment, for example, that the sides of a square are the same length. The following is a conversation between a teacher and a group of three- and four-year-olds:

Teacher:	What do you think the object behind the sheet is?
Children:	A bunny.
	It's a rabbit. It has long ears.
	It has long ears. A dog or a rabbit.
Teacher:	Does it have long pointed ears or long rounded ears?
Child:	Pointed ears. It's a rabbit.

The teacher showed the children the rabbit. Then she put a hippopotamus behind the screen.

Teacher:	What is this?
Children:	A hippopotamus.
	A rhinoceros.
Teacher:	Does it have a horn?
Child:	No, it must be a hippopotamus shape.
Teacher:	Let's look at the object. It is a hippopotamus. It has a hippopotamus shape.

The teacher put three-dimensional wooden trees behind the sheet.

Teacher:	What is this?
Children:	Tree.
	Triangle.
Teacher:	I'll turn the object around. Does it still look like a tree?
Children:	Yes.
	It's a fat tree.
Teacher:	Is this tree shaped like a triangle?
Child:	Yes.

The teacher showed the children the tree.

Teacher: I am going to put two more objects behind the sheet. Are they alike?

Children: Yes, they're triangles.
One is a block.

Teacher: Yes, they are shaped like triangles. Let's look at them.

The teacher showed the children a wooden tree, a block, and a triangular puzzle piece. She and the children talked about how the objects were alike and different. Later the teacher introduced a new object, a doll dress. The children had no trouble guessing what it was. They found a doll to wear the dress, and then the teacher put the doll behind the sheet and the children said they knew what it was because it was doll-shaped. The teacher suggested that they look at the silhouettes of all of their dolls. She and the children discussed which characteristics of dolls made them doll-shaped.

Continue to show the children different objects and talk about their characteristics. What is it about the shape of an object that helps us know what it is?

ACTIVITY 3
CHILDREN CAN BE RECOGNIZED BY THEIR SHAPES

Mathematical processes
Using geometrical relations, making comparisons, using mathematical language, and solving problems.

What you need

White bed sheet
Overhead projector or spotlight
Large mural or butcher paper
Scissors
Crayons
Pencils
Felt-tip pens

How you begin
After children have identified and compared the objects seen behind the screen (Activity 2), encourage them to stand in back of the screen and let the other children guess who they are. Speaking to groups of 6 to 10 children, say,

> You may take turns standing behind the screen and we'll try to guess who you are. I'll ask three children to stand in back of the screen. When I tap one of you on the shoulder, you can stand behind the screen.

Since there are three or more children to identify, the children must look closely for each child's personal characteristics.

The following is the conversation between a teacher and a group of four- and five-year-old children:

Teacher:	Who do you think is behind the screen?
Child:	Sarah.
Teacher:	What is it about her that tells you it's Sarah?
Child:	Her long hair.
Teacher:	Sarah has long hair. Do we have other children with long hair?
Child:	Yes, Sarah, Ann, and John.
Teacher:	Mystery Child, turn around. Let's look at you from the back.
Children:	It's Sarah. She's tall.
	Her hair is long in the back.
Teacher:	Is she taller than John or Ann?
Children:	No.
	Yes.

Teacher:	Sarah, Ann, and John, stand behind the screen and let's look at all of you together. Which one is Sarah?
Children:	In the middle. She's the tallest.
	John's hair isn't as long.
	Ann isn't as tall as Sarah.
Teacher:	John, Ann, and Sarah, come from behind the screen and let us see you.
Children:	It's Sarah. It's Sarah.
	I knew it was Sarah.

After all the children have been identified, ask two, three, or four children to stand together. Can the other children identify them?

Say to the children,

Who do you think is behind the screen?
How do you know one child is _____?
How can you tell the children apart?
Can you tell the difference between a girl and a boy?
What is the same about all of the children?
Are they people-shaped?
What makes all of them people-shaped?

Talk about the ways in which children's shapes are alike. They all have heads, shoulders, arms, bodies, legs, and feet. They are shaped like children. Say to the children,

If you traced around your bodies, would you see a child's shape on the paper?

Give the children time to answer and say,

There are paper and crayons in the art center. During learning center time you may ask someone to trace around your body.

Help the children match their tracings with their own bodies. Say to the children,

Is the tracing of your body the same shape as your body?
How can you find out?
Can you match your body to the tracing of your body?

Provide a stand-up mirror and encourage the children to look at the match between themselves and their body shapes. The children may discover that the two are not exactly the same. Ask the children,

Are they the same?
Is one taller than the other?
Why do you think that is?
Does the tracing include your feet?

Is it standing on its toes?

What position are you standing in?

What can you do so that your shape is the same as your body shape?

In one kindergarten the children drew their outlines in all sorts of positions. Their bodies and body tracings matched only when the children positioned themselves like their body tracings. The children arranged their tracings like a mural on their classroom wall.

ACTIVITY 4
SHAPES ARE IMPORTANT

Mathematical processes

Using geometrical relations, using mathematical language, and solving problems.

What you need

Crayons
Drawing paper
Pencils
Felt-tip pens
Objects in the room

How you begin

One way to better understand children's concepts of shape is to ask them to draw pictures about shapes. Speaking to small groups of six to eight children, say,

What is a circle?

Discuss the children's answers with them. Typical answers children give are "round," "a ball," "an 'O,'" and "a mirror." After talking about circles, say to the children,

Make a "circle" picture during learning center time. I'll put them on the bulletin board, and we'll look at them later.

In this study the teachers were surprised at the "round" drawings made by at-risk <u>four-year-old</u> children as well as middle-income children. Some items depicted were:

A balloon
Bike wheels
A mirror
Balls
Curly hair
A ghost circle

When the children have made "circle" or "round" pictures, you may want to ask them to draw a rectangle or triangle picture. Children must be very familiar with these shapes before they can draw a picture. Teachers should never insist that children draw a shape picture.

The next day, talk with the children about their pictures. Ask questions such as,

Why is this a circle picture?
Could it be a triangle?
Could it be a rectangle?

Help the children to understand that the shape of an object can affect its function. The following is the conversation between a group of five-year-old children and their teacher.

Teacher:	_____, tell us about your picture.
Child:	These are lots and lots of bicycle wheels.
Teacher:	They are round. What would happen if they were rectangles?
Children:	The bicycle wouldn't move.
	You would fall down.
	The wheels wouldn't turn.
Teacher:	No, we would not be able to ride the bicycle. _____, tell us about your picture.
Child:	My picture shows Mickey Mouse selling balloons at Disney World.
Teacher:	Balloons are round. Could balloons be triangles?
Children:	No, they would look funny.
	They wouldn't stay up.
	They would fall together.
	They look pretty [when they're] round.
Teacher:	Balloons are pretty. They can be filled with air or gas. Peter, what did you draw?
Child:	A plate to eat on.
Teacher:	Why do you think the plate is round?
Child:	To keep food from rolling off.

Continue to encourage the children to draw other pictures and talk about how shape determines how an object is used.

THOUGHTS ON SHAPES

Most young children distinguish between *two-* and *three-dimensional* shapes. Whether or not teachers refer to spheres and cubes will depend on the age and experiential background of the children. Some children will notice that a block has six sides that are square. When they trace around the block, however, they see a tracing of a square that has four sides and is flat. It has become a two-dimensional object. A circle and a ball are both round, but a ball is called a sphere. Rather than try to teach the names of three-dimensional shapes, encourage the children to describe how they are different from two-dimensional shapes.

OUR FAVORITE STORIES
Sequencing Events

Ordinality refers to the position of objects or events in relation to other objects or events. "I'm the first one here," "I was here before you were. You're second," "I raised my hand first," and "I was the last one chosen" are comments often heard by teachers during the school day. These remarks indicate that children are aware of ordinality, particularly the concepts of "first" and "last." Everyone wants to be first, but no one wants to be last, because it usually requires waiting for an event to happen.

Young children have more difficulty with the ordinal numbers *third* and *fourth* than with *first* and *second*. This is probably because most three- and four-year-old children can count 4 or 5 objects, but not 10. Five-year-old children can usually count 10 or more objects. Ordinal numbers are difficult for children because they do not have the same names as the more commonly used cardinal numbers. We do not say "the four boy in line." We say "the fourth boy." However, children who say, "I'm the four boy" have a knowledge of ordinal number, since they see themselves in a *positional relationship* to other children.

In most nursery-school and kindergarten classrooms, children *order* objects according to some criterion such as color, length, or width. Children also experience ordering when they sequence story pictures according to which events come first, second, third, etc. Materials available to teach *ordering* are Unifix Inset Pattern cubes, Cuisenaire rods, 1-through-10 puzzle number rods, and color tablets. *Sequencing* materials include cards that can be arranged to tell a story or describe an activity such as putting on socks and shoes. Classroom activities that stimulate the development of sequencing are following picture recipe cards, putting on clothes to go outside, following the daily schedule, and dressing and undressing dolls.

Dramatizing favorite stories is one of the best ways to involve children in sequencing activities. Children become totally involved in all aspects of a story. They listen to the story, draw pictures about the story, decide which part of the story to dramatize first, second, third, etc., choose and arrange props to dramatize the story, and take part in the dramatization.

Stories chosen for dramatization should have the following characteristics:

1. Short, uncomplicated plot (4–8 minutes required to read or tell the story)
2. Definite and clearly stated sequences of events (first, second, third, etc.)
3. Repetitious plot (repetition occurs from episode to episode and in the characters' conversations)
4. Opportunities for participation (episodes are easy to follow and language is easily learned)
5. Opportunities to hear and use mathematical language (*big, bigger, biggest; under, above, over; small, smaller, smallest; bigger than, smaller than;* cardinal number—how many? and ordinal number—which one?)

The stories *The Three Billy Goats Gruff* and *The Three Bears* meet the requirements listed above. Other stories that can be dramatized effectively are *The Turnip, The Gingerbread Man,* and *The Three Little Pigs.*

Although the activities in this chapter focus on *sequencing* and *ordinal number,* children have opportunities to use *counting* (by counting the characters in the story); *communication* (by drawing pictures and dictating stories using mathematical language); *problem solving* (by choosing and arranging props to dramatize the story); *record keeping* (by listing the steps and materials required to dramatize the story); and *spatial relations* (by placing props in the correct relationship to each other).

The following activities can be carried out with large or small groups of children. It is possible to include more than one troll and more than one small, middle-sized, and large billy goat. Children may prefer to be trees or flowers rather than goats or trolls. Therefore, it is possible to involve the entire class in the dramatization. The teachers in this study found that in the beginning dramatization usually involved everyone, but that gradually the groups became smaller and consisted of four to eight children. Eventually the children knew the story so well that they acted it out without help from the teacher.

ACTIVITY 1
LISTENING TO A STORY

Mathematical processes

Counting, using cardinal number, using mathematical language, sequencing events, and making comparisons.

What you need

A story suitable for dramatization — *The Three Billy Goats Gruff* is described in this chapter

Flannel board and figures and/or magnetic board with cardboard or wooden figures

Props — determined by the children

Costumes — determined by the children

How you begin

Choose a rendition of *The Three Billy Goats Gruff* to read to the entire group or to small groups of children. Examine the book to make sure that the goats are described as "small," "middle-sized," and "large," or "little," "middle-sized," and "big." The events in the story should follow in sequential order from the first to the third Billy Goat's crossing the bridge.

Since *The Three Billy Goats Gruff* is a familiar and popular story, the children will probably comment on the story before it is read. Examples of remarks made by children are: "I know that story. It's *The Three Billy Goats Gruff*." "The Troll is mean." "I like the little Billy Goat best." "The Billy Goat kicked that ugly Troll off the bridge."

This story provides many opportunities for using mathematical language. Possibilities for "math talk" include the number of goats, the size and number of their body parts, their order of crossing the bridge, and the location of the bridge, the stream, and the meadow.

The following describes a discussion between a group of at-risk four-year-old children and their teacher. The mathematical language used by the teacher and children is underlined.

Teacher:	Why did the goats want to go over the bridge to the meadow?
Children:	They wanted to get fat.
	They will eat and eat and get fat.
	Goats like to get fat.
Teacher:	Why were the goats hungry?
Children:	They didn't have grass.
	Goats eat grass. They didn't have any.
	They had to go up, over the bridge.

Teacher:	Where was the meadow?
Children:	<u>Over</u> the bridge.
	<u>Not far.</u>
	On the <u>other side</u> of the bridge.
	Goats have <u>two</u> horns.
Teacher:	The story says the meadow was on the <u>other side</u> of the bridge. Goats have <u>two</u> horns. <u>How many</u> legs do goats have?
Children:	They have <u>four.</u>
	Goats are animals. They have <u>four</u> legs.
	Goats have <u>two</u> eyes.
	Goats have <u>two</u> ears.
	They have <u>four</u> hooves.
Teacher:	Let's <u>count</u> the goats' hooves, eyes, and ears. Is there a hoof on each foot? <u>How many</u> hooves are there?
Child:	<u>Four.</u>
Teacher:	<u>How many</u> goats are there in the story?
Children:	<u>Three.</u>
	There is the ''<u>little</u>,'' ''<u>littler</u>,'' and ''<u>big</u>.''
	One is ''<u>little</u>,'' one is ''<u>middle-sized</u>,'' and one is ''<u>big</u>.'' There are ''<u>three</u>.''
	A <u>big</u> goat, a <u>small</u> goat, and another <u>small</u> goat.
Teacher:	Let's <u>count</u> the goats on each page of the book.
Child:	<u>One</u>, <u>two</u>, <u>three</u>.
Teacher:	Which goat crossed the bridge <u>first</u>?
Children:	<u>Littlest.</u>
	<u>Little.</u>
	<u>Small.</u>
Teacher:	The <u>little</u> goat went <u>first</u>.
	Which goat was the <u>second</u> one to cross the bridge?
Child:	The <u>middle-sized</u> goat.
Teacher:	The <u>middle-sized</u> billy goat. He is the <u>second</u> billy goat to cross the bridge.
	Is he as <u>big</u> as the <u>first</u> billy goat?
	Is he <u>bigger</u> than the <u>last</u> billy goat?
Child:	No, he is <u>middle-sized.</u>
Teacher:	Who was the <u>last</u> one to cross the bridge?
Children:	The <u>big</u> goat.
	The <u>biggest</u> goat.
Teacher:	The <u>biggest</u> goat was the <u>third</u> and <u>last</u> goat to cross the bridge. What is a troll? There is only <u>one</u> troll in the story.
Children:	Mean.
	Bad.
	A bad man.
Teacher:	A troll is pretend. It can be anything you want it to be.
Children:	He has yellow teeth.

	He doesn't brush his teeth.
	They rot.
	It changes the TV. (Child had confused the television control
	with the troll. The teacher and the children discussed the dif-
	ference between a troll and a television control.)
Teacher:	What happened <u>first</u> in the story?
Child:	The billy goat trampled on the bridge.
Teacher:	Which billy goat?
Children:	The <u>little</u> one.
	<u>Little</u> one.
Teacher:	What did the troll say?
Children:	Troll said, "Who is that crossing <u>over</u> my bridge?"
	Troll jumped <u>up</u>.
	"Come out from <u>under</u> the bridge."
Teacher:	What happened <u>after</u> the troll talked to the <u>little</u> billy goat?
Children:	The <u>little</u> billy goat said, "Don't eat me."
	The goat said, "Wait for the next goat."
	The next goat is <u>bigger</u>.
Teacher:	What happened in the <u>second</u> part of the story?
Child:	The <u>middle-sized</u> goat went <u>over</u> the bridge.

The story continued until the big billy goat knocked the troll off the bridge into the water. The teacher referred to the third billy goat's crossing the bridge as the <u>third</u> part of the story. When the big billy goat knocked the troll off the bridge, one child said, "That's the <u>fourth</u> part." Then the teacher asked, "What happened after the big billy goat knocked the troll in the water?"

Children:	The goats ate grass.
	The big billy goat crossed the bridge. He ate grass.
Teacher:	Yes. The <u>three</u> billy goats ate the grass in the meadow. That is
	the <u>last</u> or <u>fifth</u> part of the story. I'll put this book in the li-
	brary center so that you can look at it. We'll read the story
	again tomorrow.

Children usually divide this story into five parts: (1) The little billy goat crosses the bridge, with the troll under the bridge; (2) the second billy goat crosses the bridge; (3) the third billy goat crosses the bridge; (4) the third billy goat knocks the troll off the bridge; and (5) the billy goats are eating grass in the meadow.

ACTIVITY 2
RETELLING THE STORY

Mathematical processes

Using mathematical language, using ordinal number, sequencing events, and counting.

What you need

Flannel or magnetic board
Figures for flannel or magnetic board
Drawing paper
Construction paper or wallpaper
Crayons
Felt-tip pens
Stapler

How you begin

Read or tell the story again. If the story is familiar to most of the children, tell it with a flannel board or magnetic board.

Encourage the children to "talk for" the three billy goats as the story is read or told. It is not necessary for the children to recite the characters' conversations verbatim. They should put the conversation into their own words. Ask questions such as,

> What kind of voice does the first Billy Goat Gruff have? What does he say?

Repeat the questions for the middle-sized and big billy goats and the troll. Stress the ordinal numbers *first*, *second*, and *third*. This is a popular story and the children may want to hear it several times.

Place the book and the flannel (or magnetic) board and figures in the library center. Listen to the children retell the story using the book or movable figures. Encourage the children to tell the story to you and to one another. Listen for and encourage the use of mathematical language.

Place drawing paper, crayons, and felt-tip pens in the library center. When the children show an interest in the story, say,

> There are paper and crayons on the table. You can draw a picture about a part of the story you like very much. If you want to say something about your picture, you may write it, or I'll write it for you.

Regardless of their developmental stage in writing, encourage children to "write" their own stories. If they prefer, they can dictate stories for you to write for them. Some children like to draw pictures but prefer not to "write" about them. In one classroom several <u>five-year-olds</u> labeled their pictures, including writing the numerals 3 and 4. Other children gave their own interpretation of the story without changing the sequence of events. Examples of stories are:

1. A little girl is standing on the troll's bridge.
   Her toy is in the water.
   She is going to jump down and get her toy.
   I drew the toy down there [under the bridge in the picture] and it got in the water.
2. The troll is going to eat the little billy goat.
   The heart is going to bite the tail.
   (The story was written on Valentine's Day. The troll had a tail.)
3. The troll. The meadow. The goats.
   (Labeled the objects in the picture and wrote a 4 by the fourth and last episode, which showed the third goat knocking the troll off the bridge.)
4. The bridge is purple.
   The troll is under it.
   The first billy goat is crossing the bridge.
5. The little Billy Goat Gruff is on the bridge.
   This is the Big Billy Goat Gruff.
   This is the middle-sized Billy Goat Gruff.
   This is the little Billy Goat Gruff.
   (Drew relative sizes correctly.)

One kindergarten teacher made a big book with the children's pictures. She asked the children to help her sort the pictures according to the first, second, third, fourth, and fifth parts of the story. Then she asked, "How many groups do we have?" The children counted five groups of pictures. The first group showed the first billy goat crossing the bridge, the second group the second billy goat, the third group the third billy goat, the fourth group the big billy goat knocking the troll off the bridge, and the fifth group the billy goats eating grass. The children helped to number the 20-page picture book. They took turns taking the book home overnight.

ACTIVITY 3
CHOOSING THE PROPS

Mathematical processes
Counting, sequencing events, using mathematical language, using ordinal number, using spatial relations, solving problems, and making a chart.

What you need

Props chosen by children

Costumes or dress-up clothes. These may be made by the children or chosen by them from the dress-up clothes in the house center. Children may prefer not to wear costumes.

How you begin
When the children are *thoroughly* familiar with the story, say,

> We are going to dramatize, or act out, the story of *The Three Billy Goats Gruff.* What does *dramatize* mean?

Children should understand that *dramatize* means to pretend to be someone or something else and to tell a story by acting out the parts in order. Discuss the entire story with the children, referring to the various parts as first, second, third, etc. As long as the children divide the story into several time sequences, allow them to choose as many parts as they feel are necessary.

After the children and the teacher have reviewed and discussed the various parts of the story, discuss the *props* they will need to dramatize it. Make a list of the props needed for each sequence. Allow the children to choose and arrange their own props. The list may be written on a chart or a large piece of paper. Teachers who have difficulty writing on a chart while taking dictation can write on a pad and later transfer the dictation to a chart. Make sure the children understand the *purpose* of making a list: "If we write down our plans for later, we won't forget what we decided to do."

One group of nursery-school children dictated the following list:

PLANS TO DRAMATIZE *THE THREE BILLY GOATS GRUFF*

First part
    Three billy goats
    One troll
Props
    Bridge — blocks

Water — blue paper
Hill — green paper
Grass — real grass from the playground
Costumes — dress-up clothes
Daisies and fish — red and yellow paper daisies and paper fish
Second part
Second billy goat
Troll
Third part
Third billy goat
Troll
Fourth part
Third billy goat
Troll
Fifth part
Three billy goats
Hill

Allow the children to find or make the props needed to tell the story. The following is the dialogue between eight nursery-school children and their teacher.

Teacher: What can we use for a bridge?
Children: Let's use the big blocks.
                Yeah, we could stack the blocks together.
Teacher: How many blocks will you need?
Children: All of them.
                Six.
                Let's put them together and see how far they go.
Teacher: Where will you put the blocks?
Children: In the group center.
                On the carpet.
                Let's get the blocks.
Teacher: How many blocks do you think you can put on the carpet? Do
                you want to cover all of the carpet's surface or part of it?
Children: All of it.
                No, we need room for the water.
                Put the water beside the blocks. O.K.?
Teacher: What will you use for the water?
Children: Blue paper. O.K.?
                Yes, get the blocks and paper.
                We need four blocks.
                We must have five.

The children placed five blocks end to end and put blue paper on either side of the blocks for the water. They walked across the "bridge" and decided it needed to be longer, "like a real bridge." They added more blocks until they counted 10. Then the children decided to put two green Educubes together for the "hill." They cut out red and yellow daisies and taped them to the "hill." Then they placed the "hill" near the "bridge." Instead of making costumes, they decided to be "dressed-up" goats and wear clothes from the house center.

Another group of three- and four-year-old children decided to use cardboard for their "hill" or "meadow." They put the cardboard on the floor near the bridge. The teacher asked, "Will the three billy goats be able to stand together on the meadow?" One four-year-old said, "Let's stand on the cardboard. Come on." Three children stood on the "meadow" and decided they needed more space. Instead of one piece of cardboard, they decided they needed three pieces, one for each goat.

When the "meadow" was ready, they covered it with grass from the playground. They were almost finished when one child yelled, "Stop, we don't have any flowers! We have to draw flowers." The grass was removed while the children drew flowers. Then the "meadow" was again covered with grass.

The teacher asked, "Where will you put the 'bridge'?" The children decided it should be "near," but not "too close" to the bridge because "the goats need space to walk to the meadow." The children crossed the bridge several times before deciding on the best location for the bridge.

It is possible to dramatize the story outdoors as well as indoors. One playground had a small outdoor amphitheater behind a grassy hill. The children decided that there was enough space between the theater and the hill for a bridge. They found two sticks and laid them parallel to each other to represent the sides of the bridge.

ACTIVITY 4
DRAMATIZING THE STORY

Mathematical processes

Using ordinal number, using mathematical language, sequencing events, and using spatial relations.

What you need

Same materials as in Activity 3

How you begin

There are several ways to dramatize this story successfully. It is crucial, however, to allow the children to choose the characters they want to dramatize. The following suggestions for dramatization can be used with a large group of 20 to 25 children or a small group of 4 to 6 children.

1. Allow the children to choose the characters they want to dramatize. Choices may result in more than three goats and more than one troll. The number of characters in the story does not matter as long as the sequence of events remains the same. If a character is not chosen by the children, the teacher can take this part.

2. Go over the story with the children, focusing on the sequence of events. What happens first? second? third? etc. Instead of taking part in the dramatization, some of the children may prefer to be in the audience. These children may be shy or may want to see the dramatization before they participate in it. Later, most children readily choose a role.

3. Tell or read the story as the children dramatize it. Teachers should, however, encourage the children to talk for the characters. After several dramatizations, children are often able to dramatize the story without the teacher's help. They know the order of events and have no trouble following it.

ACTIVITY 5
SEQUENCING PICTURES

Mathematical processes

Sequencing events, using ordinal number, and using mathematical language.

What you need

Polaroid camera
Photographs to sequence

How you begin

During the dramatizations, take photographs of the children acting out the various parts of the story. Choose pictures that represent the events in the story. Each picture should clearly represent an episode that can be identified by the children. Most four- and five-year-olds can sequence up to five pictures. Polaroid pictures can be ordered immediately, while children still remember who took the part(s) of the first, second, and third billy goats. If children forget who was the first or second billy goat, the teacher can help them decide which picture comes first in the sequence. The third goat is easily identified since he is seen knocking the troll off the bridge. Say to the children,

> Find the picture that tells about the first part of the story. What's happening in the picture?

Continue until all the pictures are sequenced. If a child chooses a picture out of sequence, review the story until the correct picture is identified.

THOUGHTS ON SEQUENCING EVENTS THROUGH DRAMATIZATIONS

Teachers who dramatized the story with their classes felt that the warm-up activities such as reading the story, telling the story with a flannel board, and discussing the sequence of events were crucial to the success of the dramatizations. Rather than assigning roles, they preferred to allow children to select their own characters. When teachers assign roles to children, dramatizations no longer belong to them, but to their teachers. Children should be allowed to choose and arrange the props for a story. This gives them an excellent opportunity to solve problems by exploring spatial arrangements until satisfactory solutions are found.

Teachers should take advantage of the opportunities to involve children in dramatization throughout the year. When children become more familiar with acting out stories, they are capable of dramatizing longer and more involved plots. When children are familiar with the events of a story, they have no difficulty putting them in sequential order. Children can also make up their own versions of familiar stories or write or dictate original stories. Opportunities for sequencing events, using ordinal numbers, solving spatial problems, and using mathematical language abound.

OUR BOX CONSTRUCTIONS
Covering Surfaces (Area)

The activities in this chapter introduce children to the concept of *area* through the exploration of *surfaces*. Although the word *area* is not used, children touch, examine, and talk about "covering the surfaces of" boxes. While the focus of these activities is on *covering surfaces* (area), children are involved in other areas of mathematics such as *solving problems* (making block constructions); *using mathematical language* (communicating); *measuring* (exploring and matching surfaces); *using cardinal numbers* (counting the sides of boxes); and *using geometrical relations* (identifying rectangles and/or squares).

Children in this study continued to use the term *surface* whenever they covered the surfaces of other objects such as their drawing paper, the chalkboard, or tables.

EXPLORING OUR BOXES

Mathematical processes

Exploring surfaces, measuring, using cardinal number, using geometrical relations, and solving problems.

What you need

Two large furniture boxes of the same size and shape, such as refrigerator, sofa, or stove boxes.

How you begin

Place the boxes in the room and allow the children to explore them during center time.

During group time, show the boxes to the children and say,

> I brought these boxes to school today. What did you find out about them during center time?

Give the children time to answer the question. Typical answers given by nursery-school and kindergarten children are "They're big," "They're the same size," "One side is open," "We can crawl in them," and "I bet a refrigerator came in one of those boxes."

Continue by asking questions that encourage the children to think about the sides of the boxes as surfaces. Choose one box and ask the children,

> What do you think came in this box?
> What shape are the sides of the box?
> How many sides does the box have?

Allow the children to count the sides of the box by turning it around. Remember to include the top and the bottom of the box. If the children do not know that the sides are rectangles or squares (stove box), tell them. Say to the children,

> This box has six sides or surfaces. Each side is a rectangle (square).

Encourage all of the children to move their hands *across the surfaces* of the box. Say to the children,

> Does this box have two surfaces that are the same size?
> How do you know?
> Are the top and bottom surfaces the same?
> How many surfaces are the same size?

How do you know?
Let's look at the other box. What do you think came in this box?

Continue by asking questions about the second box. When you and the children have discussed the second box, place the boxes side by side and ask,

Are the boxes the same size?
How do you know?
Are the surfaces of the boxes the same size?
How do you know?

Encourage the children to compare the boxes. In order to compare boxes, children usually place them side by side or on top of each other to find out whether they match in shape and size. It will be obvious to the children that the sides or surfaces of the boxes match and that therefore the boxes are the same size.

ACTIVITY 2
PLANNING WHAT TO MAKE WITH THE BOXES

Mathematical processes

Using mathematical language, exploring surfaces, using geometrical relations, solving problems, and using charts.

What you need

Boxes from Activity 1
Felt-tip pens
Crayons
Tempera paints
Brushes
Construction paper
Glue
Newspaper
Cutting knife (sharp enough for the teacher to cut cardboard)
Chart on which to write children's plans

How you begin

Review with the children what they learned about the boxes in Activity 1. After the children have discussed the boxes, ask,

What do you want to make with the boxes?
Will you need both boxes?

One group of kindergarten children decided they needed only one box to make a bus, whereas a group of nursery-school children decided they needed both boxes to make "two houses." It is possible that a small group of children may want to make something with one of the boxes and another group something different with the other box. When the children have discussed what they want to make, say to them,

What can you use to cover the box(es)?
Do you want to cover all of the surfaces with _____?

The kindergarten children who made a bus decided not to cover the top and bottom of their box "'cause you can't see the bottom" and because "we'll cut the top off." The nursery-school children who made two houses wanted to cover "all of the surfaces" of one box with black paint, but not the bottom surface of the second box, because "it would take too long to cover the bottom with construction paper."

Continue to ask the children questions about their constructions, such as,

What else will you need for your _____?

What will you need to make the _____?

How you find the materials you need?

When the children have completed their plans, say,

I'll write your plans on this chart so you won't forget what you need. Tell me what you want me to write first.

Write what the children dictate and read it to them. Ask them if there is anything else that they want to include.

The following is a discussion about boxes between a group of nursery-school children and their teacher.

Teacher:	What do you want to make with the boxes?
Children:	Houses.
	Two houses.
Teacher:	How will you cover your houses?
Children:	Construction paper.
	Black paint.
	One house paint and one house construction paper.
Teacher:	Let's think about what you said. You told me you wanted to cover the surfaces of one box with paint and the surfaces of the other box with construction paper. Is that correct?
Child:	Yes.
Teacher:	Do you want to cover all of the surfaces of the boxes?
Child:	No. Not the construction paper box.
Teacher:	If you don't cover all the surfaces of the box with construction paper, which ones do you want to cover?
Children:	Not the bottom.
	No one sees it.
	It'll take too long.
Teacher:	Remember to cover all the surfaces, except the bottom surface. How many surfaces will you cover?
Children:	Six.
	Five. (Child counts all sides of the box except the bottom.)
Teacher:	What else do you want for your houses?
Children:	Doors.
	Windows.
Teacher:	How will you make the doors and windows?
Children:	Cut them out.
	Draw them.
Teacher:	Will you need to draw them before you cut them?
Children:	No, cut them.
	Yes, draw them first.
Teacher:	Will you cover your houses before you draw the doors and windows?

Child:	Draw the doors and windows first.
Teacher:	I'll cut the doors and windows after you draw them. Is there anything else you need for your house?
Child:	No.
Teacher:	I'll write your plans on the chart. Tell me what to write.

The chart read:

PLANS FOR OUR HOUSES

Draw doors.
Draw windows.
Teacher will cut out doors and windows.
Cover one house with black paint.
Cover the other house with construction paper.

The children covered a "big surface" of the room with newspaper so that "paint won't get on the floor." The teacher asked, "Did you cover enough floor surface so that the paint won't get on the floor?" The children said, "We'll put the box on the paper and find out." They found that the box covered part, but not all, of the newspaper. One child said, "Good, now we won't get paint on the floor."

Encourage the children to cover the entire surface of the side of a box. Questions and comments that will encourage children as they work are:

You covered all of this surface with the _____.
Have you covered the other surfaces?
Do you need more _____?
Do you need a small or large piece of paper to cover that surface?
Do you need a small or large brush to cover this surface?

In one nursery school the children noticed the uncovered spaces between the pieces of construction paper haphazardly glued on the box. Some of the spaces formed definite geometrical shapes. In order to cover the spaces, some of the children drew, cut out, and pasted on triangles, rectangles, and "almost circles." Other children cut and pasted on "big" and "little" pieces to cover the spaces. The children wanted the surfaces of the box completely covered.

When necessary, allow the children to change their plans as they work with the boxes. In one kindergarten a child wanted to draw a round door. The children liked Alice's idea because "a round door would be fun to crawl through." When the door was cut, the children had difficulty crawling through the door. They decided a rectangular door like a "real door" would be better.

ACTIVITY 3
PLAYING WITH OUR BOX CONSTRUCTIONS

Mathematical processes
Solving problems, using mathematical language, and using spatial relations.

What you need

Completed constructions from Activity 2
Materials listed in Activity 2

How you begin
During dramatic play, the children may decide that additional items are needed for their constructions. One group of five-year-olds found that using a paper plate for their bus's steering wheel was unsatisfactory. Since the "wheel" was unattached, they kept dropping and losing it. The children remedied the situation by replacing the paper plate with a mounted steering wheel from the block center.

Observe and listen to the children as they play with their constructions, and occasionally join in their play. When problems arise, make comments and ask questions to help children solve them. Questions and comments that may help children solve problems are:

What happens when you climb through the window? Is it wider than the door?

Think about it. What can you do? Is the house sturdy? What did we use to make it?

Try the square block and find out how it works.

That sounds like a good idea. Try it and find out what happens.

What materials do you need?

When children need materials that are not available in the classroom, they or the teacher may be able to bring them from home. Often children will find substitutes within the classroom. When three- and four-year-olds needed a big ladder for their fire truck, they compromised by taping a small ladder to the wall. It was no longer necessary to carry a ladder on their truck; the ladder was at the scene of the fire when the truck and firemen arrived.

One class of three- and four-year-olds wanted a table and chairs in their house. When they put a table and two chairs in the house, it immediately fell over. The children decided that the table was too big, but could not decide which of their tables should replace it. The teacher asked, "How will you know which table fits in the house?" The children answered, "We'll try all of them." Through trial and error they finally found a table that did not touch the sides of their house.

Another incident involving number and spatial relationships occurred when a group of <u>five-year-olds</u> placed six chairs tightly against the sides of their "bus." In order to "ride" in the bus, the children had to climb over the sides. One child said, "You aren't supposed to climb into the chairs. You're supposed to sit in them." The children continued to crawl over the sides of the bus until it almost turned over. Instead of attempting to solve their problem, the children lost interest in their play. In order to revive their interest, the teacher asked, "What is the problem?" The children answered, "The bus is too crowded," and "You can't walk in the bus like in a real one." The teacher said, "That's too bad. Why is the bus crowded?" The children replied, "Too many chairs." The teacher asked, "How many?" and one child said, "Six." The teacher asked, "Is six chairs too many?" Jeffrey removed a chair and then counted five chairs. He said, "I think there're still too many." Peter removed another chair and then counted four chairs. He said, "It's O.K. We can walk in the bus." The children decided that four people could ride in the bus, but not five or six.

In some situations, the teacher's questions and comments are helpful and necessary in helping children think of ways to solve their problems.

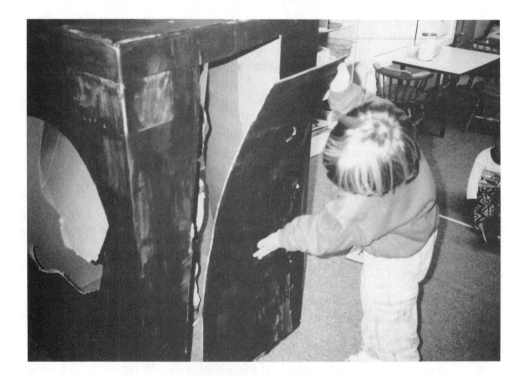

ACTIVITY 4
WRITING ABOUT OUR BOX CONSTRUCTIONS

Children enjoy drawing pictures and writing stories about their box constructions. Since making box constructions is a group project, two or more children may dictate or write a story together.

Mathematical processes

Using mathematical language, using cardinal number, and covering surfaces (area).

What you need

Newsprint *or* jumbo picture story newsprint *or* all-purpose paper on a roll
Felt-tip pens
Crayons
Pencils — jumbo and standard

How you begin

Place the paper, pens, crayons, and pencils in the writing or library center. Listen to the children's conversations as they build and play with their box constructions. Say to the children,

You may want to write stories about your constructions.
There are materials in the _____ center for you to use.

If several children have been working together, you can say to them,

Some of you may want to write a story together. _____, you and _____ have been playing together. Would you like to write a story about what you have been doing?

Children may write their stories or dictate them to the teacher. Encourage the use of mathematical language, but allow children to express themselves in their own way. Some children may want to draw or paint pictures together.

The following are stories written by nursery-school and kindergarten children:

OUR BUS

Our bus is big. It is yellow. Four children can ride to school.

THE BUS

The bus was crowded. We took out chairs. Now four children can ride.

111

Our Houses

There are two houses. One is covered with black paint. We used lots of paint. We glued paper all over the surfaces of one house. It is pretty. We live in the houses.

The Fire Truck

It is red. We painted the surfaces all over with red paint. It has two seats, two hose, and one horn.

THOUGHTS ON COVERING SURFACES

It is important for the teacher to use the word "surface" with the children and to encourage them to feel the "surfaces" of the coverings of various objects. The children in this study retained their knowledge of *surface* and continued to use it when appropriate throughout the school year.

Teachers found that it was best to allow children to come and go as they worked. This method alleviated restlessness and sparked renewed interest when the children returned to work on their constructions.

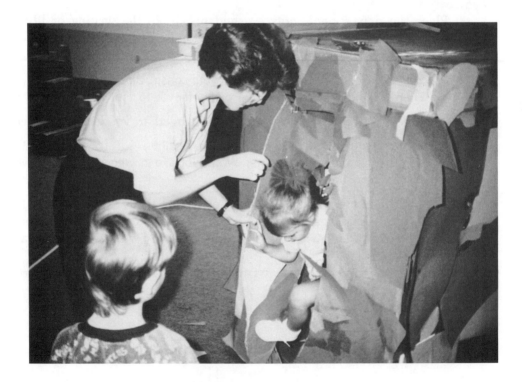

OUR MATERIALS
Volume

Young children's early experiences with objects are often associated with filling and employing containers. Comments made by children reveal their understanding of size and capacity: "I need a big box." "That box is too small for me. I can't sit in it." "We need more sand. Fill the bucket to the top." "You have more juice. Your glass is bigger than mine." (The glasses may hold the same amount of juice, but one glass "looks bigger" to the child.)

Teachers can introduce the concept of *volume* by encouraging children to explore the sizes and capacities of containers. During the activities in this chapter, children explore volume by *filling* a variety of containers with different materials, *estimating* how many of the same kind of container it will take to fill another container, and *comparing* containers to determine which one holds the most.

Containers presented to children should be familiar to them and, whenever possible, *transparent and plastic*. After a period of exploratory play, standard measuring cups and spoons can be introduced to help children discover relationships such as "This cup holds two of this little cup" and "It takes three of these spoons to fill the big spoon."

In addition to *capacity* and *size (volume)*, the activities in this chapter explore *using mathematical terms (heavy, light, amount, tall, thin, shallow, deep, more than, and the same amount); measuring* (comparing the sizes and capacities of various containers); *cardinal number* (counting the number of containers it takes to fill another container); *estimating* (predicting the number of containers it will take to fill another container); *solving problems* (determining whether containers hold as much as, more than, or less than other containers); and *using geometrical relationships* (naming and comparing the shapes of containers).

It is important to give children enough time for free play before attempting to structure the activities in this chapter. Except in Activity 5, teachers should work together with small groups of no more than six children.

ACTIVITY 1
TALKING ABOUT FULL AND EMPTY CONTAINERS

Mathematical processes

Filling containers, using mathematical language, making comparisons, using geometrical relations (naming shapes), solving problems, and measuring (*full, empty, almost full*).

What you need

A variety of containers—assorted plastic tote bins, plastic pitchers, bowls and/or cups, baskets, and small boxes. Whenever possible, include the containers' lids.

Materials found in the classroom—construction toys, small blocks, Unifix cubes, Cuisenaire rods, beads, pegs, etc.

How you begin

Choose a familiar container such as a plastic tote bin or any square or rectangular box. The container should be empty. Show the container to a group of not more than six children and say,

Tell me about this container.

Listen carefully to the children's responses. They may describe the shape of the container as "square," a "rectangle," or "rectangular." They may comment on its color, material, and texture. If the container is plastic and the children describe it as white, ask them to look through the sides and bottom of the box. What do they see? If they can see inside the box, it is transparent or clear rather than white. Some children will be able to define the container as "something to put things in." In this study, nursery-school children defined a container as "something to put food in," while kindergarten children named a variety of materials that a container can hold. After talking with the children about the containers, ask,

What can you put in a container like this one?

Some answers children give are "rubber bands," "food," "drinks," "pins," "beads," "sprinkles," "pegs," "spoons," "tools," "toys," "bugs," and "stone soup."

Talk with the children about their answers. Say to them,

Would the items fit in the container? Why? Why not?
Would you be able to carry the container if it were filled with _____?
    How? If not, why?
Would the contents spill? If yes, why do you think so?

After discussing the various items, allow the children to fill the container with the materials. Ask them,

Is the container full? How do you know?
Can you find enough _____ to fill the container?
Do you think these _____ will fill the container? How will you know?

Allow the children to fill the container with as many of the different materials as possible. After they have experimented with the materials, say to them,

Find a container in the room and bring it to the group.

A wide assortment of containers should be available. Most of the containers the children choose will be filled with materials; a few may be empty. Some containers children may choose are snack baskets, juice pitchers, plastic boxes filled with construction toys or art materials, and cups, glasses, and pots from the house center. Allow the children to describe their containers and their contents. Then ask,

Why did you choose your container?

Children's answers will vary with their age and maturity. Most nursery-school children choose containers that hold toys they have recently played with and give reasons for their selections such as "I like to string beads," "I played with the blocks," "Me and Tom made a plane with the Legos." "I brought the red basket. It's my favorite," and "Our juice pitcher holds our juice."

Kindergarten children choose containers with toys they especially like and give reasons for choosing them such as "I like to play with Crystal Climbers," "I like the big blocks best, but the box was too heavy to carry. I brought the one with Unifix cubes instead," "I chose something that wouldn't spill, like drawing paper, not paint," "I chose a box with a lid," and "I chose an empty container. It's easy to carry." After discussing the children's reasons for choosing the various containers, ask them,

Will your container hold any other materials?

Explore with the children possibilities for filling their containers with various materials. A juice pitcher and a basket may be filled with many of the same items, but pouring a liquid from a basket would be very difficult. Encourage the children to think about the relationship between their container and its contents by asking the following or similar questions:

Is your container full? Do you think you could put more _____ in it? Why? Why not?
What other objects in the room could you put in your container? Are there enough objects to fill it?

How do you know your container is full?

In one kindergarten classroom the children decided that a container was full when the material came to "the top" and "the lid fit it." Whenever possible, ask the children to find the lids for their containers. When a container is too full, this will be obvious, since the container's lid will not fit properly. Ask the children,

Will the lid fit the container when it is empty?
When it is full?
How do you know when the container is full?
What happens to the lid when the container is too full?

Continue to encourage the children to fill containers with different materials, and to use the terms *container, material, empty, almost full*, and *full*. Choose an area of the room, preferably the science or math center, in which to place the equipment. Encourage the children to play with the equipment during center time.

ACTIVITY 2
FILLING CONTAINERS

Mathematical processes

Using mathematical language, filling containers (volume), measuring, using geometrical relations, solving problems, estimating, using cardinal number, and keeping records.

What you need

A variety of *small* containers — children's shoe boxes, jewelry boxes, soap boxes, margarine or butter containers or any small food containers, and *several* sets of plastic measuring cups. Choose a few containers that are identical. Avoid any container that once held chemicals.

Materials found in the room — construction and other manipulative toys, art supplies (pom-poms, cotton balls, scraps of paper, etc.), small 1-centimeter or 1-inch blocks, Cuisenaire and/or Unifix cubes.

Felt pens

Crayons

Pencils — jumbo and standard

Manila drawing paper

How you begin

During center time talk with the children informally about the materials and containers that were placed in the Center during Activity 1. Say to them,

> If you have something you found out about filling containers that you want to share, I'll write it for you or you can write it yourself. You may want to draw a picture about it.

Some children may want to label their drawings or dictate or "write" something about them. (Accept scribbles.) The dictation can be written on paper and attached to the drawing.

Encourage a small group of not more than six children to share their drawings and/or dictated materials. Do not be concerned if there are children who do not participate through drawings or dictation; they can describe what they did and take part in the discussion. Say to the children,

> Let's talk about what you found out about the materials and containers. _____ (name of child), read us what you told me.

Children may not remember exactly what they dictated, but will usually "read" with remarkable accuracy. If there are no drawings or dictated materials, begin by saying,

Let's talk about what you found out about the materials and containers.

Encourage the children to talk about what they learned. The following comments were dictated to the teacher by <u>three-</u>, <u>four-</u>, and <u>five-year-old</u> children.

> I put four little blocks in a glass. One fell off. There were three blocks left in the glass.
> My container is big. I filled it to the top with red beads.
> Michael's box is bigger than mine. We put blocks and Cuisenaire rods in it. The box is full.
> I found some beans. I put them in a basket. They fell out the holes. I put blocks in the basket. It is full.
> I put beads in a little box to the top. It is full.
> I saw an empty pitcher. I filled it with yarn balls.

After the discussion, show the children a variety of small containers and large containers filled with Unifix cubes, blocks, Cuisenaire rods, beads, and yarn balls. Say to the children,

> Choose one of the small containers and fill it with materials from the large boxes.

Encourage the children to estimate "how many" items it will take to fill their small containers. Questions that encourage children to estimate are:

> How many _____ do you think will fit into your container? Count them and find out.
> Do you need more? How many more do you think you need?
> Do you have too many? How do you know?
> How many will you need to take out of the container?
> Will it take more _____ or more _____ to fill your container? Why do you think so?

Since the containers chosen by the teacher are relatively small, the children should be able to count the objects without much difficulty. Younger children may need more help. Nursery-school children sometimes estimate by taking a few objects from a container and saying, "This many." Other children may use their hands and count the handfuls of objects rather than each object. These are crude estimates but should be accepted by the teacher.

Encourage the children to select other small boxes and experiment with them. Place the materials and boxes in the science or math center for the children to explore during center time. Include paper, crayons, felt-tip pens, and pencils.

In order to spark interest and encourage comparisons, add a few plastic measuring cups to the containers. Observe the children during center time and encourage them to make comparisons by asking questions such as,

Which container do you think will hold more?

How can you find out?

Which container held more? less?

Can you find two containers that are the same size? How do you know they are the same size?

Will they hold the same amount of materials? How do you know?

Are the materials the same?

Are the materials different?

Kindergarten children enjoy using measuring cups either to fill containers or as containers. Comments made by them are: "I filled this bowl with two cups of blocks. It takes two cups of beads to fill the big box." "If I fill this cup _____ times with pegs, I can fill the pitcher." "These cups hold the same amount 'cause they're the same size." "I put four cups of pegs in one bowl and three cups of blocks in the other bowl. I know why that happened, because blocks are bigger than pegs." One five-year-old was asked, "Which box is bigger?" He filled one box and poured its contents into the other box. Then he said, "The other box. This one isn't full." He continued to explore amounts by filling containers and pouring their contents into other containers to find the larger container.

Through their explorations with containers and materials, children can learn that the *placement* of materials in a container can determine the number of items, or the amount, that a container can hold. In one kindergarten two children carefully placed Cuisenaire rods on the bottom of a box. They tried several arrangements but were unable to cover the entire bottom. Then one child noticed that the uncovered space was the shape of a rectangle. He chose two square blocks that fit into the rectangular space. He said, "Now the bottom is covered." The boys repeated the pattern of Cuisenaire rods and square blocks until the box was filled.

FILLING CONTAINERS WITH SAND

Mathematical processes

Using mathematical language, filling containers (volume), measuring, using geometrical relations, solving problems, estimating, using cardinal number, and keeping records.

What you need

Plastic sets of (preferably) clear measuring cups, spoons, and bowls

Small containers from Activity 2

Additional *small* containers—These should be no bigger than a child-sized shoebox

Sand

Equal-arm balance—For children who are interested in comparing masses

How you begin

During center time place additional plastic measuring cups and several plastic measuring spoons and small containers near the sand table or a large box of sand. Talk with the children informally about the new materials and containers. Encourage the children to continue their explorations with the equipment from Activity 2. Keep this equipment separate from the sand play. Say to the children playing with the sand,

> If you find out something about filling containers, I'll write it for you or you can write it yourself. You may want to draw a picture about it.

Be sure that you also offer to take dictation from the children who are exploring the containers and materials from Activity 2. Encourage a small group of not more than six children to share their drawings and/or dictations. Say to them.

> Let's talk about what you found out about the containers and materials. _____, "read" what you told me.

The following comments were dictated to teachers by three-, four-, and five-year-old children:

> Michael and I played a game. We guessed how many little blocks would fill the green box. Then we filled it up. Sometimes we were right. Sometimes wrong.
>
> I poured the blocks out of my box into a big box. It wasn't full. It was a bigger box.

It took three handfuls of pegs to fill my box.

I played in the sand. I filled five spoons with sand.

(Children wrote each numeral in these stories after a sentence was dictated.)

After the discussion of what the children found out about the containers, materials, cups, and sand, ask them to gather around the sand table. Talk with them about the measuring cups and spoons. Say to the children,

Tell me what you can about the cups and spoons.

Typical responses are, "You use them to cook," "Some are big, some are little," and "The spoons are little."

Most children will stand the cups side by side and then match the bottoms and tops. They may place the spoons inside each other to see whether they are the same size.

Tell the children that these are measuring cups and spoons and that they are used in cooking. Encourage the children to fill their cups and spoons completely with sand as they explore filling the various containers. Encourage the children to predict the number of cups and/or spoons it will take to fill their containers. Older children can write the answers in numerals, and younger children can draw pictures of the containers to help them remember their estimates. Some children will want to draw and write. Some will not be able to write all or some of the numerals. Teachers can, however, write the numerals for them or encourage them to draw the number of cups or spoons. Since the containers are small, most children will be able to count the number of cups or spoonfuls of sand it takes to fill them. If not, teachers can help the children count.

Children who have previously played with measuring cups and sand should arrive at more accurate estimates. Ask questions to encourage more realistic estimates, such as,

Look at your container. What shape is it? Is it the same size as the other containers that are _____?

Is it smaller?

Is it larger?

Is it the same size?

How many cups of sand do you think it would take to fill your container? How many spoons?

The children may use the spoons and cups as both containers and measuring devices. Some children will be able to make comparisons between and among the items. One five-year-old said, "I know two cups of sand will fill this bowl. I learned that before." Ask the children questions that encourage experimentation and making comparisons, such as,

What shape is your container?

If you use the small spoon, how many spoonfuls do you think it will take to fill the cup? How many large spoonfuls?

Why do you think it takes more small than large spoonfuls to fill the cup?

How many spoonfuls of sand would it take to fill the largest bowl? The smallest bowl?

Which container holds more sand? How can you find out?

In one kindergarten a child said, "I know how we can find out which container has more. Put them on the balance." John used the balance to compare the two containers. Other interested children began using the balance to compare containers and made their decisions based on the results.

Place other measuring cups and spoons, bowls, and other containers near the water table or a large container of water. Include only water-tight containers. Encourage free play at this center. Keep the sand and water play separate.

Encourage the children to "write" and draw about what they find out.

FILLING CONTAINERS WITH WATER

Mathematical processes

Using mathematical language, filling containers (volume), measuring, using geometrical relations, solving problems, estimating, using cardinal number, and keeping records.

What you need

Water table *or* large container filled with water
Containers (water-tight only) from Activity 3
Measuring spoons and cups
Equal-arm balance — for children who are interested in comparing masses

How you begin

Talk informally with the children about the materials at the water table. Allow them to continue their explorations with the sand, but keep this equipment separated from the water play.

Say to the children playing at the water and sand tables,

> If you have something you found out about filling containers, I'll write it for you, or you can write it yourself. You may want to draw a picture about it.

Encourage a group of not more than six children to share their drawings and/or dictations. Say to them,

> Let's talk about what you found out about the containers, sand, and water. _____ (child's name), read us what you told me.

The following were dictated to the teacher by three-, four-, and five-year-old children.

> It took two cups of sand to fill my container. It took three cups to fill Drew's container. His container holds more.
>
> I like the baby measuring spoon. It takes lots of spoons of sand to fill a little box.
>
> I used the equal-arm balance to find out which container holds the most sand.

After the discussion with the children, ask them to gather around the water table. Follow the same procedure and questioning techniques as in Activity 3. Allow the children to continue their explorations with the sand and water for as long as they are interested. After a few days, say to a small group of children,

> We are going to wet the sand with water. How is wet sand different from dry sand?

Typical responses given by children are, "It stays together when you squeeze it," "You can press it together," "It feels wet," "Dry sand pours," "Dry sand falls apart, but wet sand stays together," and "You can make things with wet sand." Say to the children,

> Wet sand will stay together when you press or pack it. Let's wet the sand.

Allow the children to pour water on the sand until it is firm but not soupy. Continue exploration with the wet sand and containers. The children will find that wet sand takes the shape of the container. Observe the children as they press or pack the sand in their containers, turn the containers upside down, and then remove them from around the molded sand. Ask the children,

> What shape is the container?
> What shape is the sand?
> Are the container and the sand the same shape? the same size?
> How do you know?

To answer the above questions, most children will place the container over the mound of sand and say, "They're the same. See."

Encourage the children to continue these explorations and to "write" and draw pictures about what they find.

MAKING A SCRAPBOOK ABOUT FILLING CONTAINERS

Mathematical processes

Measuring, filling containers, using cardinal number, using mathematical language, estimating, solving problems, and keeping records.

What you need

Children's drawings and dictation from Activities 2, 3, and 4
Scrapbook *or* construction paper *or* wallpaper for the cover of the book
Stapler

How you begin

Say to the entire group of children,

> I'm going to put the drawings and the written information you gave me in a scrapbook. Let's look at all the drawings and papers I have for your scrapbook.

Show and read some or all of the children's work. Put the children's materials in a large scrapbook or make a cover for a large book. Read the book to the children and then place it in the library center.

Encourage parents and visitors to read the book. If children make further discoveries with the containers and materials, allow them to draw pictures about or dictate what they found out. Add this information to their book.

Most groups of children will want to "name" their book. Some titles that children chose for their books are: *Our Information Book, Our Book About Filling Containers, What We Learned,* and *Containers in Our Room.*

THOUGHTS ON FILLING CONTAINERS

Teachers should be careful not to structure the activities in this chapter too much. The purpose of the activities is to *fill various containers* with materials and *use the terms material, container, filled, empty, more than, less than,* and *the same amount* accurately. *Teachers must allow for free play with the materials.*

Except in Activity 1, it is important that none of the containers be larger than a child's shoebox. Some teachers found that children tired and quickly lost interest when they were asked to fill large boxes with materials.

Teachers should encourage, but not pressure, children to draw or "write" about their discoveries. This can be done informally throughout the day.

10 OUR HOUSES

Spatial Relationships and Counting

One of the favorite activities of young children in preschool and kindergarten classrooms is building with blocks. When told by an adult, "Tell me about your building," children often say, "It's a house." If it's an elaborate house, they may describe the function, size, and position of each room. Typical comments made by children about their block houses are: "I made a house for me and my mommy." "My house has two rooms." "I have a garage." "See, this room is little; this one is big." "I put the living room next to the kitchen."

Children may live in apartments, duplexes, trailers, detached houses, or other types of dwellings. Regardless of where they live, children's homes are very important to them. They think of their homes as an extension of themselves and may ask their teachers, "Do you know where I live?" Children often give misleading (but, for them, accurate) directions to their houses: "You know where the fire station is? Go pass it and there is my house." "You go down a hill and my house is at the bottom." "Do you know Billy? I live near him." "My house is close to that big lake."

Both boys and girls enjoy building block houses and playing with miniature houses or dollhouses. Today many classrooms have dollhouses, and blocks are considered essential pieces of equipment. Children learn more about homes, families, and daily living through block and dollhouse play. They often "play out" real-life family situations that help teachers learn more about their attitudes, interests, and feelings. Most often, children make up situations that reflect their experiences and interests.

The activities in this chapter help children to develop spatial understandings by playing with and building houses. Children decide which boxes fit together to build their houses, how "high" and "long" to make them, how much furniture will fit into the rooms, how to select boxes to make furniture, and where to place the furniture.

Although the activities focus on *spatial relationships* and *counting* (finding out how many rooms are in a house and how many people in a family); children have opportunities to use *measurement* (exploring the "surfaces" [area] of boxes); *geometry* (describing the shapes of boxes and fitting them together); *problem solving* (choosing boxes to make houses and planning strategies for making them); *classification* (placing furniture that belongs together in one room); and *communication* (discussing houses with teachers and classmates, writing or dictating stories about houses, and drawing pictures of houses).

The following activities should be carried out in small groups of no more than four nursery-school or six kindergarten children. Teachers who helped to develop the activities found that they could help children best during learning center time or small-group time, with teachers and aides taking turns working with various groups.

The length of time spent on these activities depends on the age and interest level of the children. One kindergarten teacher estimated that her class would be involved for two or three weeks; however, the children's interest lasted for four weeks. They continued to use boxes to make houses and other buildings throughout the year.

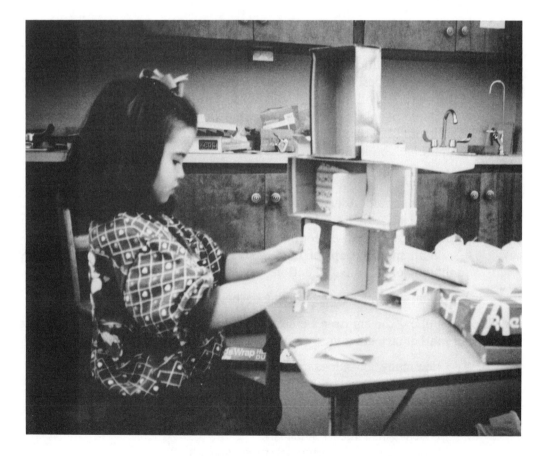

TALKING ABOUT HOUSES

The purpose of talking with children about doll- or block houses is to encourage the *use of mathematical language* and an *awareness of spatial relationships,* including *separation, proximity, order,* and *enclosure.*

The aide should supervise the learning centers so that the teacher can move around the room listening to the children's conversations as they play and build with blocks.

Mathematical processes

Using spatial relations, counting, classifying, solving problems, and using mathematical language.

What you need

Hardwood dollhouse (open on one side) *or* floor or tabletop dollhouse (open on all sides) *or* wooden apartment house (open on one side) *or* plastic dollhouse (open on one side) *or* Duplo dollhouse (permits changing design of house) *or* unit blocks

Multi-ethnic doll families—dollhouse family set, wooden family set, Duplo people, or other miniature people

Dollhouse furniture or other miniature furniture

Small-block building set(s)

How you begin

Teachers should observe children as they play with dollhouses and build with blocks. Although this chapter centers around dollhouses, children's block constructions, preferably houses, can be used in all of the activities.

With small groups of four to six children, gather around an empty dollhouse or block construction. Say to the children,

What can you tell me about the dollhouse (block construction)?

Follow the children's comments with questions that focus on the use of mathematical language. Questions that may be asked are:

How many floors does the house have?
Which is the first floor? the second floor?
How many rooms are in the house?
Are they the same size? How do you know?
Which is the largest? smallest?
How are the rooms separated from each other?
Is a large room beside a small room?
How many windows are there? doors?

How many people do you think can live in the house? Could more
than _____ people live here?
How can the rooms be used?
What kind of furniture can you put in the _____ room?

Make a list of the furniture to put in each room. There may be two,
four, six, or more rooms, depending on the type of dollhouse or block
house construction. Dollhouse furniture, Duplo furniture, or any kind
of miniature furniture may be used. Tell the children that they will each
have a turn to put the furniture in the house. When the furniture is in
the house, say to the children,

Is there enough space in the rooms for the people to move around com-
fortably?
Do we need to remove any of the furniture?
Did we use all of the furniture?

If the answer is "No," say,

Can we use any of the furniture we didn't use? Will the rooms be too
crowded if we add more furniture?

Continue to guide the discussion until the children are satisfied with
the arrangement of the furniture. Each group of children will have different ideas about the rooms and the furniture. Later they will play with
the dolls and houses, arranging and rearranging the furniture. They may
talk to and for the dolls in their play.

Usually children pretend that the people are a family—father,
mother, and children. Sometimes children from single-parent homes
choose only one parent for their pretend family. One child chose a
mother and referred to an invisible father who was "not at home."

In one kindergarten the children played with their dollhouse for
several weeks. During learning center time, the teacher and six children
gathered around the dollhouse, and the following dialogue ensued:

Teacher:	Let's talk about our dollhouse. How many floors does it have?
Children:	Two.
	A downstairs and upstairs.
Teacher:	What is this floor called? (Points to bottom floor.)
Children:	Bottom.
	First floor.
Teacher:	What is this floor called? (Points to second floor.)
Children:	Second floor.
	Top floor.
	Last floor.
Teacher:	This is the first floor and the top floor is called the second floor. It is also the last floor in the house. Some houses have three or more floors.

Children:	My house has an attic.
	I don't have an attic.
	I do.
Teacher:	Yes, some houses have attics. Let's count the rooms on the first and second floors.
Child:	Three and three. (Children counted with their eyes.)
Teacher:	How many altogether?
Children:	Six. (They counted with their eyes.)
	Three and three is six.
Teacher:	Three and three is six. Let's count the doors and windows? (The children and teacher counted 5 doors and 16 windows.) Why do you think there are more windows than doors?
Children:	'Cause people have to look outside.
	Houses need lots of light.
Teacher:	How are the doors and windows different?
Children:	Doors touch the floor.
	Doors are bigger so you can get out.
	You have to see out windows. They're high.
Teacher:	Are the windows higher than the doors?
Children:	Yes.
	No.
	We need to measure.
Teacher:	What can we use to measure?
Children:	Paper strips.
	My finger.
	Ruler.

The children measured the height of the windows and doors. They found the strips of paper and the ruler were more accurate than their fingers. They learned that the doors and windows reached the same height on the walls but that the doors "began at the bottom" and were "longer than the windows." They decided that all of the windows were squares and that the doors were rectangles.

The teacher continued the discussion:

Teacher:	Are all the rooms the same size?
Children:	No.
	Some are bigger.
	I see some bigger.
	These rooms are big and these are small. (Child pointed to the rooms.)
Teacher:	These rooms are bigger than these rooms (pointing to the rooms). How do you know?
Children:	You can tell by looking.

	The small rooms are under each other and the bigger rooms are under each other. See.
Teacher:	That's right. What can we put in the rooms?
Children:	Doll furniture.
	Put the kitchen downstairs.
	Put mother and daddy upstairs.

The teacher and children talked about each room and its use. Then the teacher made a list of the furniture the children wanted to place in each room. After the furniture was in place, the teacher continued:

Teacher:	How many people can sit at the table?
Children:	We'll get the dolls.
	I think four.
	There's four chairs.
Teacher:	Will more than four chairs fit around the table?
Children:	No.
	Let's put the people around the table. Four people can sit at the table.

The teacher continued to ask questions and the children estimated the number of dollhouse people that would fit in a specific room or on a piece of furniture. There were three sets of families — white, African-American, and Asian. Some of the questions the teacher asked were:

Do you think more than one doll can sleep in the bed?
Which bed do you think the children can sleep in? How many children do you think can sleep in the bed?
Is there room on the couch for all of the people to sit?
How many people do you think can sit on the couch?

The teacher encouraged the children to experiment with the dolls and furniture.

In one nursery school, four children who built a block house talked with their teacher and two interested classmates about the construction:

Teacher:	Tell me what you can about the house.
Children:	It has three rooms.
	It's wood.
	There is a door and windows.
Teacher:	Let's look at the rooms. Are they the same size?
Children:	No.
	This room is big. This one and this one are little.
	There is a big room.
Teacher:	How are the rooms separated from each other?
Children:	This is a wall. I made it with blocks.

	Blocks.
	Block walls.
Teacher:	Are the rooms close to each other?
Children:	Yes.
	Yes. You can walk from here to here to here.
Teacher:	They are near, or close, to each other. Is one room closer to the big room than the other?
Children:	Yes.
	You go to this room and this room (pointing to rooms). This room is first, next to the big room.

Teacher and children continued talking about the size of the rooms. One child said, "We need a point for a roof." The children discussed a pointed roof but decided there was no way to build it with blocks. They talked about a flat roof but abandoned the idea when they realized that they could not see the rooms if they put a roof on the house. The children built the furniture for the house with small colored blocks. They furnished a living room (with a block couch and chair), a bedroom (with a block bed), and a kitchen (with a block sink, table, and chairs). The children continued to play with their house and later built another block house. Soon there were several block houses. The teacher met with each group to talk about their houses.

In carrying out this activity, it is important to encourage the children to try out their ideas about houses. By observing the results of their efforts, children learn to evaluate and adjust their strategies until they are satisfied with the results.

ACTIVITY 2
WRITING ABOUT HOUSES

Mathematical processes

Counting, using mathematical language, using cardinal number, using spatial relations, and solving problems.

What you need

Same materials as in Activity 1
Felt-tip pens
Crayons
Pencils — jumbo and standard
Newsprint *or* jumbo picture-story newsprint *or* all-purpose paper on a roll

How you begin

Listen to the children's conversations as they play with the dollhouses and block constructions. Most children will choose miniature people that represent family members and will act out situations that are realistic. Sometimes children make up fanciful stories about the dolls and families. Encourage children to share their stories by asking questions such as:

How many people are in the family?
How many children?
What are they doing?
What are they saying to each other?
What will they do today? tomorrow?

Continue by asking questions that follow the children's description of events. Most children will describe what is happening now, but a few will talk about past or future events.

Place paper, felt-tip pens, crayons, and pencils in the writing or library center. Say to the children,

You may want to write stories and draw pictures about the dollhouse families (block constructions). There are materials in the _____ Center for you to use.

The children may want to write their stories or dictate them to the teacher. Encourage the use of mathematical language, but allow children to express themselves in their own way. Some children may want to write several stories. These may be made into a book, or the children may want to write in journals.

Stories written or dictated by <u>five-year-olds</u> in a kindergarten were:

My Family

Mother is cooking dinner. Father is going to the pool with Zack and Terrell. There are eight people in the family. Helen is a four-year-old. There are lots of lights in the house.

The Big House

The people are sitting in chairs and a girl and a boy are laying in bed. It is a big house. It has six rooms. One person is watching T.V. Five people are sitting in the chairs.

A Family

The rooms are all different. The people are different. There are 2 boys and 1 girl in the family. There are 3 children. The boy says, "I like you." The girl says, "I don't know you." (Child wrote numerals.)

The New House

5 little girls are watching T.V. The mother is sitting down and 1 boy is sitting. They just moved into the house. There are 6 rooms. They are going ice skating and to the fair. (Child wrote numerals.)

Stories written by <u>four-year-olds</u> were:

Halloween

There are four people in the family. Halloween night they go out to trick or treat. When they get home from trick or treat they go to bed. But first they eat supper.

People in the House

Five people live in the house. 1 child is in the dining room and 2 children are on the water bed. (Child wrote numerals.)

Stories written by <u>three-year-olds</u> were:

The Family

Mother, Daddy, baby live in the house. There are three rooms. The baby is three years old.

Family

The mother makes dinner. The boy and girl like pizza. They go to nursery school.

ACTIVITY 3
LOOKING AT HOUSES

Mathematical processes

Using spatial relations, using mathematical language, counting, using ordinal number, and using cardinal number.

What you need

Paper plates, paper, and clothespins *or* small notepads
Drawing paper
Pencils — jumbo and standard
Felt-tip pens
Crayons

How you begin

With a clothespin, fasten several sheets of paper on a paper plate. The paper may be used to draw pictures and the paper plate to support the paper. Notepads may be used instead of the paper plates.

This activity using the paper plates or notepads is appropriate for five-year-olds. The same activity can be carried out with four- and three-year-olds without using plates and paper or notepads to record information. Say to the children,

> We are going to take a walk around our school to look for houses or other buildings. When you see a house or building you like, draw it on the paper. When you have filled the first page with pictures, turn it over and draw on the next page. What kinds of buildings do you think you will see?

Since the children are familiar with their surroundings, they will be able to describe some of the houses and other buildings they see. Whether children see only houses, only other buildings, or both will depend on the location of their school. In most localities, they will see both. During the walk, ask children questions that focus on *spatial relationships*, such as:

> How many stories does the house have?
> Does it have a first (second, third) floor? How do you know?
> How many windows can you see? Why do you think there are so many? few?
> How many doors can you see? Is there a front door? Do you think there is a back door?
> How many buildings can you see if we stand here? Why do you think the _____ is next to the _____?

How are the houses separated from each other?

Why do you think the house is separated from the street by a fence? yard?

Are other buildings separated from the street? How?

When the children return to the school, talk with them briefly in small groups about what they saw on their walk. If you are working with five-year-olds, encourage them to refer to their drawings to remember what they saw. After the discussion of their walk, say to the children,

You may draw a house that you saw or would like to live in. If you want me to write something for you, I will. You may want to write it yourself.

One three-year-old drew a house and then wrote several pages about it in scribbles. She "read" what she had written to her teacher. Some children preferred to label the various parts of their pictures, while other children wrote or dictated stories. Some of the houses children wished they had were:

A SAILBOAT HOUSE

A sailboat house   1,000 bathrooms
100 rooms   1,000 kitchens
100 people

A HOUSE I WANT

The people went inside and had to build a ladder to crawl up on the roof. One person lives in this house—me.

THE HOUSE

There are as many rooms as window panes—24. There are three floors.

THE BERENSTAIN BEAR HOUSE

This is the house, the Berenstain Bear House. Five bears. They have a big, big house with smoke coming out every day. They have a big chair for Daddy. They take naps on the floor.

One school in a small community was surrounded by businesses such as a grocery store, a fast-food restaurant, and a service station. The teacher and children talked about what they saw in relationship to their school: "Which building is nearest our school? Farthest away? How do you know? Which door in our building would we use to walk to the _____? Is this the shortest way?"

These four-year-olds also toured their school and talked about the functions of the different rooms. The children were particularly interested in the bathroom. Why were there so many toilets and sinks? They decided it was "because we have a lot of children in our school." They toured the cafeteria and asked, "Why are there so many tables and chairs?" They decided it was "because there are a lot of hungry people." There were big pots and spoons, "'cause people at school eat a lot of food."

A kindergarten class toured their 100-year-old, four-story building. The children were amazed at the number of stairs to climb, the long halls, and the many rooms. One child said, "It's a very tall building. No man can climb to the top, except Hugo men [workmen who helped during Hurricane Hugo]. They climbed up to the top and fixed the lights. There are lots and lots of rooms. There are fourteen. Anyway, that is as far as I can count."

ACTIVITY 4
MAKING HOUSES

The size and complexity of the houses children make will vary with each group of children and with each child. Some of the houses children made had three stories, six rooms, a garage, and a doghouse; others had one story with an all-purpose room. Boxes were glued together vertically and horizontally to make the houses and the various rooms. Furniture was made out of small boxes and decorated with pieces of fabric. People were made by drawing faces on tongue depressors and dressing the figures in fabric clothing. A few children twisted pipe cleaners into people and glued on paper faces. Some children worked for three or four days on their houses.

Mathematical processes

Using spatial relations, counting, classifying, using geometrical relations, solving problems, measuring, and using mathematical language.

What you need

Boxes with lids—a variety of small boxes (shoe-, soap, jewelry, etc.). You will need at least 10 boxes per child. Parents can help to collect boxes. Omit any box that held medicine or chemicals.

Glue

Scraps of construction paper and materials such as cloth, wallpaper, felt, etc.

Scissors

Clear and masking tape

Stapler

Tongue depressors

Pipe cleaners

Small spools

Yarn balls

How you begin

Choose an assortment of boxes to discuss with the children. Boxes should include shoeboxes and packing boxes that are slightly larger than shoeboxes, as well as smaller boxes such as jewelry and soap boxes. Save very small boxes, such as paper-clip, rubber-band, and pencil boxes, for making the furniture.

With small groups of four to six children, talk about the boxes. Say to the children,

We are going to make houses out of boxes. Here are some boxes you can use to make a house. Let's look at the boxes together.

Choose a shoebox to talk about. Ask questions such as,

What do you think comes in a box like this?
What shape is the box?
How could you use this box to make a house?
Would you need more than one shoebox?
What other kinds of boxes would you need? What kinds that are smaller
    than a shoebox? larger than a shoebox?
Let's look at the other boxes.
Are there any boxes the same size? How do you know?
What shape are the boxes? How could you fit them together?

After you have talked about each kind of box, say,

Think about the kind of houses you want to make.
How many stories do you want?
How many rooms?
When you decide, you may choose the boxes you will need to make your
    house.

Allow children to begin work on their houses immediately. Talk with
each child about the number and kind of boxes he or she needs. Ask
questions such as,

How many stories do you want?
How many boxes will you need?
Will they be the same size? Different sizes?
How will you put the boxes together?

Encourage the children to experiment with the boxes. They may
change their minds about the arrangement of the boxes as they experiment. Accept their decisions. Some children will make two-story houses;
others one-story houses.

In this activity, the type of commercial dollhouse found in a classroom did not appear to influence the kinds of houses the children made.
In one classroom, with the exception of two children, four-year-olds
made one-story houses. Although they played extensively with their two-
story, eight-room dollhouse, they used a single shoebox or larger box for
their houses. They usually divided the space into two or more areas.
With the exception of four children, these children lived in one-story
houses with three or four rooms.

The children made furniture and placed it in specific areas to identify
the various rooms. For example, a bed, a table, and a bathtub were
placed in areas designated as the bedroom, the kitchen, and the bathroom. Instead of using another box for a second story, several children
visually divided the top of the first story box into rooms by placing
furniture in designated spaces. The children drew windows, which the

teacher cut out. They made curtains and rugs out of fabric. Several children cut out flowers and trees and glued them to the outsides of their houses.

Children who lived in one- or two-story houses with several rooms made two- and sometimes three-story houses. A story might include two small boxes and one larger box to indicate two small rooms and one large room. Some children drew doors between rooms. They also drew windows and front, side, or back doors. The teachers cut out the windows and doors for them. The children sometimes used small boxes for garages, which were sometimes separated from and sometimes attached to the houses. Doghouses were small boxes placed nearby. One five-year-old used a small box for a mailbox. She made a newspaper out of a rolled-up piece of paper.

A few children may choose to make buildings other than houses. One four-year-old made a hotel with many bedrooms. He had recently stayed in a hotel for the first time.

After the children have worked in small groups to make their house, talk with each group about making furniture. Show the small boxes and ask,

What kind of furniture do you want to make for your house?

Which box could you use to make a(n) _____? a(n) _____?

Could you make a _____ by gluing some of the boxes together? Which ones?

What shapes are the boxes? Are they the same size? How do you know?

How will you put them together?

Put out scrap materials, spools, buttons, and glue, etc. Allow the children to choose the boxes they need to make furniture. Most children will want to decorate their furniture with scrap materials. During this activity some children made pillows, bedspreads, curtains, rugs, lights (from yellow paper), pictures, and doorknobs.

While the children are making the furniture for their houses, ask questions such as,

Will the _____ fit in the _____ room? Will there be space for more furniture?

Do you need a large or small bed? What kind of box will you need to make it?

Will you need more than one box to make the _____?

Many children will spend three or four days making their houses and furniture. As they play with their houses they may decide to add more furniture and rooms.

WRITING ABOUT OUR HOUSES

Most children are very proud of their houses and enjoy writing about them. They may write or dictate more than one story as their play with houses evolves.

Mathematical processes

Using mathematical language, using spatial relations, counting, and using cardinal number.

What you need

Newsprint *or* jumbo picture-story newsprint *or* all-purpose paper on a roll
Felt-tip pens
Crayons
Pencils—jumbo and standard

How you begin

Listen to the children's conversations as they play with their houses. Most children will play with other children, making up stories as they go along.

Place paper, felt-tip pens, crayons, and pencils in the writing or library center. Say to the children,

> You may want to write stories about the houses you made. There are materials in the _____ center for you to use.

Children may write their stories or dictate them to the teacher. Encourage the use of mathematical language, but allow children to express themselves in their own way. Some children will write several stories. These may be made into a book, or journals may be made available to the children.

Stories written by <u>five-year-olds</u> in a kindergarten were:

MY FAMILY

Brother and sister are sleeping in the beds. Sister is trying to get the books off the shelf and she did. Dad, mother, sister, and brother are watching T.V. There are four people in my family.

MY FAMILY

There is 1 baby sister and 2 brothers in the family. They all live in the same room. The rooms are all different. They have an invisible dad. The mom cooks at home. (Child wrote numerals.)

THE FAMILY

People are in the house asleep. There are ghosts and witches there. There are six rooms in the house.

MY HOUSE

My house is big. My house is pretty. I have three doors. My house has a bed. It has a kitchen. It has two closets.

MY DOLLHOUSE

I like my house because it has rainbows on it. I have lots of friends in the neighborhood. I live beside Marquis. I made three people.

Stories by four-year-olds were:

THE BEACH

There are no people at the beach. It is closed. It will open on Sunday. It is closed on Monday, Tuesday, Wednesday, and Thursday when I am in school. It is open on Friday and Saturday. Today it is closed because I am at school. [This child surrounded her house with brown paper to make a beach.]

MY HOUSE

Open the door and go up the stairs. There is a sea-brick chimney. A lot of smoke goes out the chimney. There are three rugs. The big one is pink. The triangular one is by the stairs. The triangular rug is teal green. [This child's father is an architect.]

A MOTOR HOME HOUSE

It can pick up cars. People don't live in here now because the tire went out. It has four good tires and is worn out!

THOUGHTS ON MAKING HOUSES

Most children greatly enjoy making houses. Teachers found that it was better to allow several groups of children to make houses at the same time. This method reduced waiting time when children were anxious to begin.

It is very important to talk to children individually about their houses and to encourage them to write stories about them. When teachers listen to children talk about their houses, they become more aware of children's mathematical language, which enables teachers to ask more thought-provoking questions and to make appropriate comments that lead to further learning.

11 OUR CITY

Spatial Relationships and Mathematical Language

As a follow-up to Chapter 10, "Our Houses," or as part of a unit such as "Community Helpers" or "Neighborhoods," children can build a city with the houses and other buildings they have made. Children focus on *spatial relationships* as they arrange houses, hotels, schools, other buildings, and parks in relation to one another; plan and arrange roads that are winding or straight; and place trees, bushes, animals, and people near, far away from, beside, inside, or outside houses and other buildings.

In addition to spatial relationships, children are involved in other areas of mathematics such as *using geometrical relationships* (identifying the shapes and sizes of buildings); *using cardinal number* (counting the number of buildings, people, cars, trees, etc.); *communicating* (using mathematical terms such as *curved, straight, rectangular, surface, edge, number, up* and *down*); *classifying* (placing animals in zoos or parks, and vehicles in garages, airports, or fire stations); *measuring* (identifying the boundaries of their city); *estimating* (estimating distances between and among buildings); *using area* (determining the amount of surface needed for the city and its parts); and *solving problems* (making decisions about when, where, and how to make and place objects in the city).

Children in this study were as enthusiastic and excited about making cities as they were about making houses.

ACTIVITY 1
PLANNING OUR CITY

Mathematical processes
Making a chart and using spatial relations.

What you need

Houses and buildings made during the activities in Chapter 10
Chart paper and stand *or* chalkboard
Felt-tip pen *or* chalk

How you begin
Children's *conception* of a city will vary from group to group and from child to child. Children from rural communities learn about cities through books, excursions, films, and television. All children will include in their cities the things that are important to them. Each year a kindergarten class in a small community visits a large city to attend a circus performance. These children included a circus in their city.

When the children have completed their houses, say to them,

You can make a city with your houses. What else will you need for your city?

Write the children's suggestions on a chart. They may think of something that you have not anticipated or are afraid they cannot make. Be assured that they will think of ways to make whatever they suggest. Their idea of perfection may be very different from that of adults. When the children have completed their list, read it to them and ask,

Is there anything else you want to include in your city? I can add it to the list.

Add anything the children suggest to the list. The list will be modified whenever the children decide to add something new to or omit something from their city.

Here is the list of suggestions made by one nursery-school class:

WHAT WE NEED FOR OUR CITY

houses	schools	tunnel
trees	church	dogs
buildings	water	cats
grass	railroad	Cherry Park
fire station	pavement	bird nest
roads	subway train	beach
zoo	doors	clothes
people		

LOCATING OUR CITY

Mathematical processes

Using mathematical language, covering surfaces (area), using spatial relations, estimating, and solving problems.

What you need

Houses and any other buildings made during the activities in Chapter 10
Area in the room for a city

How you begin

Allow the children to decide where to put their city. It may be necessary to move furniture or even a center for one or two weeks. The length of time spent on making and playing with the city depends on the group and the individuals in the group. During group time, say to the children,

> Where can you put the city? You need space for your houses and the other buildings you plan to make.

Continue to ask questions to help the children think carefully about the location of their city. Encourage them to *estimate* the size of the area they will need for their houses.

Questions that will help the children to estimate are:

> Do you think there is enough space in the _____ area for the houses and buildings you plan to make?
>
> How do you know?
>
> How can you find out?

It will be obvious to the children when a space is too small. Their buildings will be too close together or will not fit into the space. Another area must be chosen or the present site enlarged by moving furniture or by incorporating another center.

One group of kindergarten children suggested tracing around the bottoms of their houses, cutting the shapes out, and placing the patterns in the middle of the room. When the patterns were placed on the floor, the children quickly saw that there was no room left to walk from center to center. They put the patterns in the group center and decided that there was enough room in the center for their city. This left enough space in the middle of the room for group time.

In one nursery school the children devised a way to show the boundaries of their center. The following is the dialogue between the children and their teacher:

Teacher:	Where can we put our city?
Children:	On the rug.
	In the house center.
	Let's put it here (group center).
Teacher:	The floor of the house center is carpeted. Will your houses cover the surface of the rug?
Children:	Yes.
	It's too small for all of them.
	Put them here in the group center.
Teacher:	Is the surface of the group center large enough for your houses and other buildings?
Child:	Yes.
Teacher:	How big is the group center?
Children:	Big.
	We can measure.
Teacher:	What can we use to measure?
Child:	Put string around it.
Teacher:	Get the string and measure the center.

One child put the string around the edge of the rug indicating the boundary of the center. The children agreed that there was room in the group area for their city. The teacher continued the discussion:

Teacher:	What is outside the string?
Child:	Part of [the] room.
Teacher:	What is inside the string?
Child:	Group center.
Teacher:	The string shows the boundaries of the area we call group center. Where will you put your houses?
Children:	Next to each other.
	Inside the string.
	No, like a city. All around the rug.
Teacher:	How will you know how far apart to put the houses?
Child:	Put them this far apart. (Holds thumbs horizontally with tips touching and fingers straight up.)
Teacher:	Do you want to measure that way? (Holds hands like child.)
Children:	Yes. We can do that.
	Not your hands. They're too big.
Teacher:	My hand is bigger than your hand. Are your hands the same size?
Children:	Yes.
	No.
	Almost.

The children put their hands together and decided they were the same or almost the same size. Then they put their houses on the rug.

Most of the children remembered to use their hands to measure the distance from their house to another house. They decided it was all right if the houses were not exactly the same distance apart.

The size of the area will either hamper or encourage creativity. When space allows for expansion, children's conceptions of buildings and cities will be expressed in their work. If necessary, teachers should be willing to rearrange their rooms temporarily while children pursue their interest in making a city.

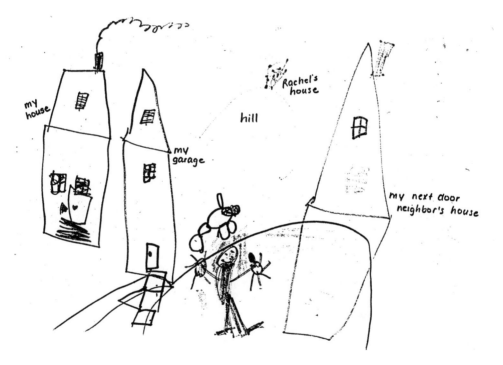

ACTIVITY 3
MAKING OUR CITY

Children tend to be very enthusiastic about making a city. All of the three-, four-, and five-year-olds in this study participated in the activities. The three-year-olds were particularly interested in making trees, bushes, birds, and people. Older children enjoyed creating zoos, parks, circuses, and schools. One four-year-old chose two identical boxes to represent the restrooms in the city park. On one box she placed a sign "Boys" and on the other a sign "Girls." She said, "No one will know they're bathrooms." Her teacher said, "Think about it. What can you do?" Later Katie said, "Look, I made toilet paper. Now everyone will know they're bathrooms." She had rolled pieces of paper and put them in each box.

Mathematical processes
Using mathematical language, using spatial relations, solving problems, using geometrical relations (shapes), measuring, and estimating.

What you need

Small boxes of all kinds
Construction paper
Manila drawing paper
Crayons
Felt-tip pens
Glue
Spools
Buttons
Scraps of fabric
Wallpaper
Tongue depressors
Pipe cleaners

How you begin
Place the materials on tables or on shelves where art materials are kept.

When the children are satisfied with the placement of their houses, show them the chart with the plans for their city. Read the list to the children and ask,

Which of the things on your list do you want to make today?

When the children choose an item to make, put a check mark beside it. Show the children a few of the materials available to them and say,

What could you use to make a _____ (tree, bush, people, etc.)?

Accept each child's suggestion and discuss the various materials that can be used to make the item. Encourage the children to work together whenever possible, to choose their materials, and to find an area in the room to work. Ask the children,

Do you need anyone to help you?
How many of you are making the same thing? Would you like to work together?

The teacher or aide should circulate among the children as they make items for their city. Questions to ask children when appropriate are:

How can you fit the _____ together?
Is this the way you want it to look?
What shape is the _____?
Where do you plan to put the _____ (school, church) in the city?
Will it be close to the _____ (park, zoo)? far away from the _____ (house, park)? How will you separate it from the _____ (house, store)? Is there enough space? How will you know?
What other materials can you use?
How can you make the _____ (dog, boy) stand up?

Encourage the children to work with the materials until they are satisfied with the results. One three-year-old decided to make a "people" for his house. He chose a tongue depressor and drew a face on one end. The teacher suggested fabric for the clothes, but John preferred to "draw" (color) the clothes. He wanted "his man" to stand up. He tried various ways to make the tongue depressor stand, but all failed. Then he looked through the boxes of construction toys, took out a bristle block, and stuck the end of "his man" in the block. John said, "Look at my man. He's standing up." Then he put "the man" inside his house.

Most children will pretend that they live in the houses. One kindergarten child who could "write" made signs to identify her classmates' houses. Another five-year-old added three boxes to her house to make her nursery school. She called the largest box the playroom, the two middle-sized boxes the "motor room" (activity room) and bathroom, and the smallest box the kitchen. Each room was identified with small-box furniture, fabric, and buttons.

One group of four-year-olds wanted a sun, a moon, and birds. They made the items out of paper and hung them from the sprinkling pipes along the ceiling. They decided that the moon and sun could hang side by side because the moon is there even when you cannot see it.

Several three- and four-year-olds became involved in making roads to and from buildings, parks, zoos, schools, and airports. One child drew yellow lines in the middle of the black construction-paper roads. Then the children connected the roads to the houses, but did not extend them to the zoo, the airport, the school, or the park.

The teacher asked questions that helped the children understand the importance of extending the roads. Some of the comments made and the questions asked by the teacher were: "You made many roads from one house to another. Are your roads straight, zigzagged, or curved? Which road is closest to _____ house? How will you go to _____ house? Which road will you take? How will you know which direction to go? How will you go to the park? Will you walk? Drive?" The children realized that they needed roads to connect all parts of their city. They included a detour and a Fix-It Shop on the road to their park.

Before the end of each day, talk with the children about their city. Encourage them to describe the things they made and how they relate to the other features of the city. One five-year-old was concerned because blocks were used to "fence in" the zoo animals. He said, "You can't see the animals." His teacher asked, "What do you want to do?" Robert said, "I'll fix it." He moved the rectangular blocks, replaced them with cylindrical blocks, and placed them at intervals. Now everyone could see the animals.

At the beginning of each day, go over the plans for the city with the children and check the items they want to make. Continue until all of the items are checked. There may be a few items that they choose not to make. This should be their decision.

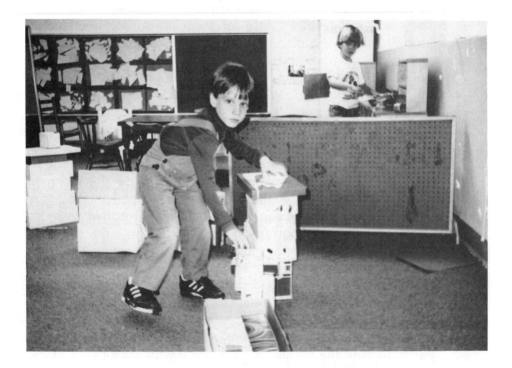

PLAYING WITH OUR CITY

Children enjoy playing with their city. Some children will make additional items for the city; others will play with whatever they find in the city. Children may add roads, buildings, trees, and people as the need arises.

Mathematical processes

Using mathematical language, solving problems, measuring, using geometrical relations (shapes), and estimating.

What you need

Same materials as in Activity 3

How you begin

The teachers who were involved in these activities found that they could clarify and extend children's ideas best by becoming involved in their play. One nursery-school teacher joined a small group of children who were driving toy cars up and down the city roads. Cameron wanted to drive his car to the school, but the road ended abruptly in front of a house. His teacher said, "The road ended. What do you want to do?" Cameron said, "I'll make a detour around the house." He cut a strip of black construction paper, placed it at a right angle to the road, made a sign that said "Detour," and placed it next to the road. The teacher asked, "Why is there a detour?" He replied, "The road is broken." She asked, "Is your road straight or curved?" He said, "Straight, but it turns here." Four-year-old Philip wanted black paper to make "more roads," but Crystal had the last piece of black paper. Philip asked, "Are you making a road?" She replied, "Yes, I'm going to cut this paper." Philip said, "I'll fold it in half and we can both make a road." Crystal asked, "Will they be the same?" Philip folded the paper and tore it in half. Then he placed one half on top of the other half. He measured them carefully, handed one half to Crystal, and said, "Here, they're the same." One four-year-old wanted a sandbox and a merry-go-round on the park playground. She cut out two paper circles and placed them in the park. The teacher asked, "Which one is the merry-go-round and which one is the sandpile?"

One kindergarten group wanted to add more caged animals to their zoo. They asked the teacher, "What can we do? We want more animals, but there isn't any room." The teacher said, "Let's look at the area the class chose for their city." The children and the teacher walked around the city to determine its boundaries. They decided they needed "a little more space for the animals." During group time the children showed their classmates the amount of space they needed. The class agreed that the zoo cages could be placed "a little" outside the boundary of the city.

Although groups of children and their cities will differ, teachers can ask general questions that apply to most groups:

Do you have enough space?
How much surface will it cover? Show me.
What can you do?
Which materials do you think will work best?
What shape do you want it to be?
What is the shortest way to the _____ from the _____? the longest way?
Is the road curved, zigzagged, or straight?
Do you want the _____ near the street or away from the street?
Do you want your _____ close to the _____? Where will you put it?
What else do you need for your _____?

The teacher's comments and questions will depend on the complexity of the children's cities. Teachers should allow children to play with their cities as long as they are interested.

After eight days, a nursery-school teacher suggested the children take their city apart. Several children said, "No, we want to play with it." Their play continued for three more days.

ACTIVITY 5
WRITING ABOUT OUR CITY

Children are enthusiastic about writing and dictating stories about their city. They may prefer to "write" individually or in small groups.

Mathematical processes
Using mathematical language, using spatial relations, using cardinal number, and using ordinal number.

What you need

Crayons
Felt-tip pens
Pencils — jumbo and standard
Wallpaper and/or construction paper
Manila drawing paper and/or easel paper
Polaroid camera
Stapler

How you begin
Place the writing materials in the library or writing center. Journals may be included and the covers made with wallpaper or construction paper. The pages and cover can be stapled together.

If possible, take photographs of the children making items for and playing with their city. Talk about the photographs and encourage the children to dictate or write stories about them. Often two or more children appear in a photograph and want to dictate or write a story together. These stories and photographs can be placed in a scrapbook or teacher-made book.

Sometimes children prefer to draw pictures and dictate or write stories about them. Some five-year-olds may want to keep a record of the growth of their city by drawing pictures and writing in a journal. Most journals are from three to five pages. In one nursery school three children drew maps of their city.

Reinforce the children's interest in the photographs and in their drawings and stories by displaying them on the bulletin board. Appropriate questions to ask children to encourage them to think about their pictures are:

I like your picture. Tell me about it.
I like this photograph. Tell me what is happening in the picture.
What are you doing? What is _____ doing?
I think I see the _____. Am I right? Tell me more about it.

Do you remember how you made it?

You placed the _____ beside the _____. Why did you decide to place them close to each other?

After you have discussed the pictures with a child, say,

Your picture is interesting. Tell me about it and I'll write it for you, or you can write it yourself.

Always encourage children to "write" themselves, even when they are in the scribbling stage. They should always write their own names as best they can. Stories written by one or more children were:

Our City

This is our city. It is wonderful. It has 22 houses. It has buildings, trees, curved and straight roads, a zoo, and a park.

Our Road

We made a road for the cars and buses. It is straight. It is nice.

Our School

We have a big old wall around the school. It will stay up. We will glue it. We are going to paint this side of the wall. This side is already painted. One side is for Christmas decorations and the other side is for a trash can.

My House in the City

The house has magic steps and a magic roof that can change into anything in the world. It turns stuff into something else.

It has a magic door that changes people into Halloween costumes.

It has four stories. Upstairs is where the tools are. The next floor is the pretend playroom and school room and the next floor is the real playroom and the bedroom. The toys are up there. The bottom floor is the den.

Pipes

I put pipes in the city. They got broken. I fixed them with tape.

The Playground

I made a slide and rainbow climber for the playground. I cut strips of paper and stapled them down. They stood up like a real climber. I made a sliding board. I folded a strip of paper and stood it up.

THOUGHTS ON SPATIAL RELATIONSHIPS

Teachers who participated in these activities were surprised at the children's interest in making a city. The opportunities for problem solving and learning about spatial relationships are boundless. The teacher's awareness of the possibilities for learning more about spatial relationships is crucial.

12 OUR PATTERNS
Patterns and Relationships

To recognize a pattern, children must examine its parts for similarities and differences. They learn to recognize patterns by looking at what came before and what comes next in the pattern.

Rather than asking children to repeat a pattern, the activities in this chapter give them the opportunity to make their own patterns. In one school the teachers learned that when four- and five-year-old children understood "what comes next" in relationship to "what came before," they had no difficulty understanding and making patterns.

In addition to enabling children to recognize and create patterns, the activities in this chapter explore other areas of mathematics, such as *using mathematical language* (terms such as *same, different, before, after,* and *repeat*), *solving problems* (creating patterns from a variety of materials), and *sequencing* (arranging pictures in order).

FINDING PATTERNS

Mathematical processes

Making patterns, using mathematical language, and solving problems.

What you need

No materials are needed for this activity.

How you begin

Choose a three-word body sequence to say with the children. Sequences such as head–eyes–shoulders and chin–elbows–feet are easily remembered since these body parts are familiar to children.

Repeat the body sequence with the children several times. Then begin again and stop after naming the first or second body part. Say to the children,

What comes next?

Say the sequence again and encourage the children to supply the beginning, middle, and end of the sequence by asking,

How does it begin?
What comes next?
Are we saying the same thing over and over again?
We are making a pattern. Patterns repeat themselves. They tell us what comes next.

Give the children the opportunity to think of their own sequences. Some five-year-olds taught five- and six-word body sequences to the other children. Most four-year-olds thought of three-word body sequences. The children understood the idea of a pattern as a continuation of "what came before."

In some groups the children noticed the patterns on their clothing and on other objects in the room. The following is the conversation between a teacher and a group of five-year-olds.

Teacher:	A pattern tells us what comes next.
Child:	There is a pattern on your dress. It's red, black, red, black.
Teacher:	That's right. My jacket has a pattern. What other patterns do you see?
Child:	The lights. Look, they make a pattern.
Teacher:	What is the pattern? How does it begin?
Children:	Line–light, line–light, line–light. It goes on and on across the room.

	I see another pattern. The calendar, number–space, number–space, number–space.
Teacher:	Can you see any other patterns from where you are sitting?
Children:	Yes. Windows.
	Susie's dress.
	The rug.
	The tile.

The teacher asked the children to describe the sequences of the patterns they saw.

Play the sequence games as long as the children are interested, encouraging them to talk about the relationship between "what came before" and "what comes next." Ask them to look for and describe the patterns they find in their room. Ask questions such as,

What comes first?
What comes next?
If the pattern went on and on, what would come next?

ACTIVITY 2
MAKING PATTERNS

Mathematical processes
Making patterns, using mathematical language, solving problems, and keeping records.

What you need

Familiar objects to make patterns with — Unifix cubes, colored blocks, Legos, Crystal Climbers, pegs and pegboards, beads and string, etc.
Paper
Crayons
Felt-tip pens
Paints
Brushes
Finger paints

How you begin
Place a few familiar manipulative objects on the tables in the math center and paper, crayons, and felt-tip pens in the art center. Children can use a variety of equipment and materials found in the room to make patterns.

After playing a few sequence games, say to the children,

> Look around the room and find something you can use to make a pattern. You can use any of the objects you find.

Encourage the children to use a variety of materials to make patterns. In this study most of the three-year-olds were not ready for the concept of patterns. In one group of five-year-olds, two children did not participate at first. After watching the other children make patterns, they became interested. Whenever a child makes a pattern, ask questions such as:

> Where does your pattern begin?
> What comes next?
> Where does your pattern end?
> How would your pattern look if it kept going on and on?

Children in this study were enthusiastic about finding and making patterns. In one kindergarten five-year-olds used mural paper to draw around the large and small blocks they were using to make a pattern. Knives–spoons or knives–spoons–forks were popular patterns often traced by the children to take home. The children in this study never tired of making and finding patterns. They often made patterns at home and shared them at school.

Examples of patterns made by <u>three-</u>, <u>four-</u>, and <u>five-year-olds</u> at school were:

Alternating lines and circles drawn in shaving cream
Alternating handprints in finger paint
Alternating play-dough animals — lion–dog, lion–dog, etc.
Alternating cookie cutter arrangements — heart–circle–square, heart–circle–square, etc.
Repeating sponge painting shapes
Alternating Unifix cube arrangements
Alternating sticker arrangements

It is important for teachers to provide many familiar objects and materials. New, less familiar objects and materials are not appropriate since children want to play with and explore the new items.

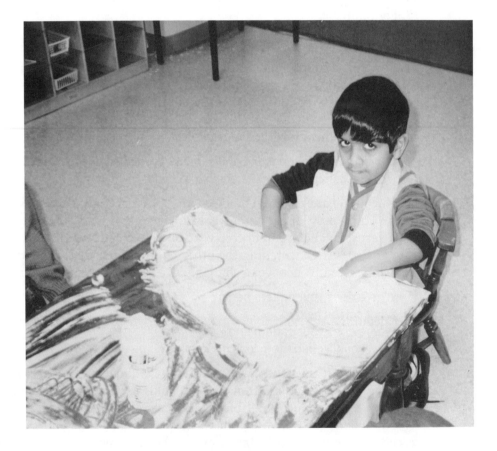

RECORDING PATTERNS

Mathematical processes

Making patterns, using mathematical language, solving problems, and keeping records.

What you need

Paper plates
Notepaper (9″ × 12″)
Clothespins
Crayons
Felt-tip pens

How you begin

Children can find patterns outdoors as well as indoors. When the children are on the playground, ask them to look for and describe the patterns they see. Say to the children,

> While you're on the playground, look for patterns. Tell us about the patterns you find.

Encourage the children to describe their patterns. Some four- and five-year-olds had no difficulty finding patterns. They saw patterns in fences, bricks, climbing apparatus, windows, and tricycle tires.

When the children are able to identify patterns outdoors, bring them back indoors. Place a few sheets of paper on each paper plate, fasten it with a clothespin, and distribute these "notepads" to the children along with crayons and pens. (You can provide them with real notepads instead, if you prefer.) Say to the children,

> When you see a pattern outdoors, draw it on this paper. There are several pages to draw on.

Encourage the children to talk about their drawings and write the names of their patterns. Five-year-olds were particularly skilled at using inventive spelling to identify their patterns. The following are examples of their work:

Bic — pattern showing spokes of bicycle
H T — house, tree, house, tree
B P B — bricks, pavement, bricks, pavement
FLYERS — white, pink, white, pink (flowers)
BEREKYRL — brick patterns on the brick wall

RRICS — brick, space, brick, space
ROOD BLOKC — road, block, road, block

Some teachers were surprised at some of the patterns the children discovered such as the arrangement of boards on their toy shed, the yellow broken lines in the paved transportation area, the trees and flowers, the bars on the climbing apparatus, and the colored flowers that alternated between white and pink.

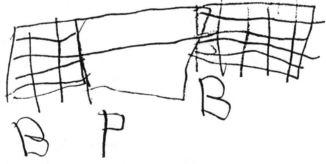

ARRANGING OUR PICTURES

Mathematical processes

Making patterns, using mathematical language, solving problems, sequencing, and keeping records.

What you need

Photographs of three or four distinctly different daily events
A low board to put pictures on
Masking tape for placing on the backs of the photographs (using masking tape enables children to change the position of the photographs)
Polaroid (*or* standard) camera

How you begin

Take three or four Polaroid photographs of the children doing distinctly different activities (for example, arrival at school, learning center time, group time, outside time, and snack time). The pictures should all be taken on the same day, preferably the day before they are shown to the children.

Tape the photographs on the board in random order and say to the children,

> Let's look at the photographs together.

Talk with the children about each photograph and then say,

> Which of these photographs shows what we do when we come to school in the morning?
> _____, put the photograph on the board.
> Which of the photographs shows what we do next? and next? Who can arrange these photographs in order?

Allow a few children to order the pictures and then say,

> Are the photographs in order? Let's look at them.

When the children have checked the photographs, say,

> Are there any other photographs we need to take?

Some groups of children will be satisfied with three or four photographs. Others will suggest additional photographs to complete the school-day sequence.

When the children have decided whether to take more photographs or concentrate on three or four, say to them,

How many photographs will we take tomorrow?

Will the photographs look like these photographs?

Which photograph will we take first?

The next day, take the photographs with the children's help. Encourage the children to order them under the photographs taken the day before. Ask questions such as,

How did you know which photograph came next?

How are the photographs in the second row like the photographs in the first row?

What are we doing in the fourth photograph?

Does the photograph tell us what activity came before? Which one comes next?

Are the photographs like a pattern? How?

If we took photographs tomorrow, would we know how to arrange them?

The following is the conversation between a teacher and a group of five-year-olds.

Teacher:	If we take photographs tomorrow, will they look like these photographs?
Children:	No.
	Yes, sometimes.
	Some things would be the same.
Teacher:	Would we take the photographs in the same order?
Child:	Yes.
Teacher:	Can we tell by looking at the photograph on the board which one we should take second?
Children:	Yes, we can. In learning center time we do the same thing every day.
	It's just like a pattern.
Teacher:	How is it like a pattern?
Child:	It tells what comes next.
Teacher:	Yes, our schedule helps us know what to do next.

Continue to take pictures as long as the children are interested. Stress the *sequence* of the photographs by asking what came before and what comes next.

ACTIVITY 5
PATTERNS IN THE SCHOOL DAY

Mathematical processes

Making patterns, using mathematical language, solving problems, and keeping records.

What you need

Chart or board with photographs taken in Activity 4

How you begin

The purpose of this activity is to help children understand that their school day has a pattern and that patterns can help us. Most older four-year-olds and five-year-olds will be able to answer the question, "How do patterns help us?" Ask the children,

> If we took more photographs, would they show the same activities as the photographs on the board?
> Would they tell us "what came before" and "what comes next"?

The following is the conversation between a teacher and a group of four-year-olds.

Teacher: How did you know where to put the photographs?
Child: I put them in order.
Teacher: Do you think we'll take the same kind of photographs tomorrow?
Child: Yes, every day is like a pattern.
Teacher: What part of the day is the same?
Child: Arrival, play time, group—everything, we know what to do because we do it every day.

Most groups of children enjoy taking photographs. When children take photographs, ask questions such as:

> How will we know where to put the photograph?
> Can you match it with another photograph?
> What could we use instead of photographs to show what we do each day?

In this study the above question elicited some unusual answers. Four-year-olds thought of drawing pictures while some five-year-olds thought of using symbols.

The following is a conversation between a teacher and her kindergarten children.

Teacher: What could we use in place of photographs to show what we do each day?

Child:	Draw pictures.
Teacher:	Yes, we could. You may draw pictures during learning time. We can put them on another board.
Child:	That's too many pictures to draw.
Teacher:	Would the same person have to draw every picture?
Child:	No, lots of people could draw the pictures.
Teacher:	What else could we use?
Child:	Symbols.
Teacher:	What kind of symbols?
Child:	I don't know.
Teacher:	What is a symbol?
Child:	The American flag is a symbol.
Teacher:	A symbol stands for something. What does the American flag stand for?
Child:	Our country.
Teacher:	That's right. It stands for America. Can you think of other symbols?
Child:	Words.
Teacher:	Yes, words are symbols. Your names are symbols. They stand for you. (She opened a big book.) Look at the page in this book. There are lots of symbols—words. This says "Mrs. Wishey Washey." Her name stands for her.
Child:	We could use words for our board.
Teacher:	What words would you use?
Child:	Arrival, snack, nap time—you know.
Teacher:	You may look at the photographs on the board and use words to describe them. If you need help writing the words, I'll help you. Would anyone else like to use symbols? Pictures are symbols too.
Child:	I'll draw pictures.

Although the children knew very little about symbols, they were able to think of ways to use them in place of the photographs.

Some children will continue drawing pictures; others will draw only a few. Encourage the children to put their pictures under the photographs on the board or, if it is too crowded, a separate board. A few children may want to use symbols — usually words — in place of pictures.

Useful questions to ask children are, "Why are patterns important?" and "How do they help us?" In this study some of the answers showed an insight into the meaning of patterning. Some of the answers given by four- and five-year-olds were:

Patterns help us to know what to look for.
When you know about patterns, you can look for some more.

Patterns tell us what comes next.
Patterns help us know what to do.

THOUGHTS ON MAKING PATTERNS

Children are enthusiastic about making patterns when they are allowed to use their own ideas and materials. Most children will continue to make and to find patterns in their environment.

Although each preschool and kindergarten program follows a schedule, there are events such as birthdays and field trips that may change the scheduling. Children realize that patterns in their lives can sometimes be broken.

13 OUR PLAYGROUND

Spatial Relationships and Making a Map

Children as young as <u>four</u> begin to draw maps; these are usually road or treasure maps. Their road maps show mostly lines going in many directions, while most treasure maps include both lines and pictures. These differences are probably due to the fact that many young children are exposed to road maps and have seen picture maps in the movies, on television, and at children's theme parks.

Children's first maps are *concrete* and *tangible*. They make houses, roads, trees, and people with blocks and create hills, roads, and houses in the sand. After a common experience, such as a field trip, children may draw or paint pictorial maps depicting what they have seen. To make *semipictorial maps*, children use more *symbols* such as color to represent water and trees. *Base maps* include the barest details drawn by the teacher while the children fill in other details, usually in pictorial form (Charlesworth & Lind, 1990).

In this chapter the children make a simple base map after many experiences building houses (Chapter 10) and making a city (Chapter 11). In addition to *spatial relations*, the activities in this chapter explore other areas of mathematics such as *using mathematical language* (terms such as *square, rectangle, close to, beside,* and *enclosure*); *measuring* (comparing the sizes of the various pieces of equipment); *estimating* (predicting the closer of two objects to another object); and *solving problems* (determining where to place equipment and where to plant bulbs on a map of the playground).

ACTIVITY 1
PLAYING ON THE PLAYGROUND

Mathematical processes

Using mathematical language, using spatial relations, estimating, and solving problems.

What you need

Playground equipment
Polaroid camera

How you begin

In order to make a map of the playground, teachers must carefully consider the possibilities for map making suggested by the physical properties of the playground. The parameters of most playgrounds are defined by fences, low walls, or shrubbery. The amount and kinds of stationary equipment will depend on the location and type of school.

The purpose of this activity is to help children become more aware of their playground, its physical properties, the relative positions of the stationary equipment, and the concept that symbols can be used to represent real objects.

When you are supervising the playground, stop and talk with the children who are playing on the equipment. Ask them:

What is the name of this equipment?
How do you use it? Show me.
What other equipment can you see?
Is the equipment far away? Is it near? What's it next to?
What else do you see? (the fence, the building, the trees, the bushes, etc.)
Are they on the playground? Outside the playground? Beside the fence? Outside the fence? Enclosed by the fence?

Talk to the children about relative positions such as "near," "close to," "beside," "far away," "next to," "in back of," "in front of," etc. Help them to understand that the equipment is either *portable* or *stationary*. Ask questions such as,

What do we do with the sand toys before we go inside? We can move them because they are portable.
What equipment stays on the playground because it is fastened down or too heavy to move? It is called stationary equipment.

Use the terms *portable* and *stationary* with the children. Children like big words and will use them when they talk about their playground.

Continue to talk with the children about their playground and the

169

relative positions of the objects they see. When the children are familiar with the playground and stationary equipment, ask them to stand against the fence (wall, shrubbery) outside their classroom door. Ask them to describe the equipment closest to them.

> What is the equipment closest to us?
> Turn your head toward the _____ (building, street, shed, etc.). What do you see?
> How do we know which equipment is closest to us?
> How can we find out which is closest? Is it the _____ or the _____?

Accept the children's answers. Preschool children may say, "It looks closer." Some answers children have given are: "It looks like the sandpile is closer," "I'll walk to the jungle gym and count my steps," and "We can get a rope to measure."

Use the children's suggestions for estimating the distances between them and the objects. There will be children who are not interested in this activity. Kindergarten children may want to measure distances using their footsteps and/or a string or rope.

Tell the children you are going to take Polaroid pictures of the stationary equipment. Whenever possible, allow older preschool and kindergarten children to take the pictures with your help. Five-year-olds took pictures of the following stationary equipment on their playground: seesaw, playhouse, rabbit hutch, sandbox, sliding board, climbing posts, climbing bars, tire swings, trampoline, and storage house.

ACTIVITY 2
PLANNING OUR MAP

Mathematical processes

Using mathematical language, using spatial relations, estimating, and solving problems.

What you need

Large sheet of paper (approximately 48″ × 48″ or 48″ × 60″; the size will depend on the shape of your playground)

Heavy paper such as mural or butcher paper

Photographs taken of the playground equipment

How you begin

Mark a large sheet of paper with a boundary that the children can use as a point of reference. In one preschool the teacher marked the edges of the paper with green X's to indicate the fence around the playground and red X's to show the gaps in the fence where the school building enclosed the playground.

You should have a definite purpose for making the map. If possible, wait until the children are beginning to make maps in their play and/or a situation arises where the use of a map would be particularly helpful.

In this study the children found that maps of their playground could help them to locate treasure on a treasure hunt; choose where to play first on the playground; pick locations for new pieces of equipment; and find places to plant bulbs for next spring.

With small groups of not more than six children, introduce the concept of a map. Ask the children,

What is a map?
Is there more than one kind of map?

Accept the children's answers and talk about the importance of maps in helping to locate places of interest to children and adults. Discuss the various kinds of maps that are familiar to the children and tell them that they are going to make a picture map together. The following is the conversation of a group of three- and four-year-olds and their teacher.

Teacher: We talked about planting crocus bulbs around the playground for next spring. Do you think we will be able to remember where we planted our bulbs?

Children: Yes, I'll remember.
I want my bulb next to the sandbox.
Let's write it down.

	Where do we put our bulbs?
Teacher:	Each of you could keep a record of where you planted your bulb. What might happen if all of you decided to plant your bulbs at the same place?
Child:	It would be crowded.
Teacher:	It would be hard for the children to find their plants. If we had a map of our playground, each of you could find a place to plant your bulb. I have a large piece of paper we can use to make a map. What shape is the paper?
Children:	A rectangle.
	Like our playground.
Teacher:	Yes, the paper is a rectangle. I drew green crosses around the edge of part of the paper to show our fence and red *X*'s to show our building. I drew two lines to show the door to our playground. I'm going to put the paper on the floor and you can sit in front of it. How can we make a map with this paper?
Children:	Draw pictures on it.
	Draw the stuff on our playground.
	Write words.
Teacher:	How will we know where to put the pictures and words?
Children:	Think about it.
	Look at our pictures.
	We know where things go.
Teacher:	Let's look at our photographs. Here is one that shows the first thing we see when we go out the door to our playground.
Children:	Our climbing bars.
	It's the climbing bars.
Teacher:	Where can we put this photograph?
Children:	Near the door.
	Close to us.
Teacher:	Jane, put the climbing bars where you think they belong.

Occasionally the teacher asked the children to close their eyes and think about the stationary equipment and its location. When all of the pictures were placed, the teacher removed them from the map and repeated the same procedure with the other groups of children. The last group of children wrote the names of the equipment under the photographs.

The making of the picture map will vary with each group of children. One teacher of four-year-olds found that the children did not want to use the photographs, but were ready to draw the pictures of the equipment immediately. When photographs and drawings are used, remember to ask the children to write the names of the equipment under them. Accept the children's inventive spelling.

ACTIVITY 3
MAKING A MAP

Mathematical processes

Using mathematical language, using spatial relations, estimating, solving problems, and keeping records.

What you need

Picture map from Activity 2
Crayons
Felt-tip pens
Chart paper

How you begin

Working with small groups of not more than six children, show the children the map with the photographs of the stationary equipment. Say to the children,

> Let's take the photographs off the paper and draw the equipment. If you cannot remember the location of some of the equipment, the names on the paper will tell you where to draw it. You may want to work in groups of two or three to draw the equipment.

Accept the children's representations of the equipment. Some pictures will closely resemble the actual objects; others will be crude representations. The accuracy of the drawings will depend on the stages of art development the children are in.

Continue to work with small groups of children until all the drawings are completed. While the children are drawing, ask questions such as,

> Is the _____ a large piece of equipment? Is it as big as the _____? Is it behind the _____? in front of the _____? Is it next to the _____? Will you have enough space to draw it?

In this study the children often drew trees, shrubbery, flowers, grass, and/or sand toys on their map. The teachers talked to the children about the *spatial relationships* between the objects by asking questions such as "Is the tree behind the fence? on the playground? near the sliding board? How many trees do you see from the climbing bars? Are the trees close together? far apart?" Whenever the children were uncertain about the placement of the objects on their map, they took the map outside and compared it with what they saw on their playground.

Help the children understand that their drawings are *smaller* than the real playground equipment and that their placements are *estimations* of the relative positions of the real objects. Talk about the differences in *perspective* between looking down at the map of their playground and looking directly at the playground. If your school has more than one floor, have the children look at their playground from a second- or third-floor window.

ACTIVITY 4
CHOOSING WHERE TO PLANT OUR BULBS

Mathematical processes
Using spatial language, using spatial relations, estimating, solving problems, and keeping records.

What you need

Map from Activity 3
Round sticker for each child (preferably of the same color)
Shovel for planting bulbs
Water

How you begin
The purpose of this activity is to help the children find a location on their map that will show where they want to plant crocus bulbs. They must be able to see the relationship between the location of stickers on the map and the location of the bulbs on the playground. Teachers can help children make this transition by asking questions that help them visualize their playground while looking at their map.

Working with small groups of not more than four to six children, ask the children to sit along the edge of the map so that they are facing the drawing of the door leading from their classroom to the playground.

Tell the children that they are going to choose a place on the map to show where they want to plant their bulbs. Say to them,

Think about what your bulb will need to grow.

Give the children a chance to answer and then ask,

Will it get enough rain? snow? sun? Will it be in the way of the other children?

The following is the dialogue between a teacher and a small group of three- and four-year-old children.

Teacher: Where is a good place to plant your bulbs?
Child: In the sandbox where it can get rain.
Teacher: It will get rain and sun in the sandbox, but what could happen to the bulb?
Child: It will get dug up.
Teacher: Can you think of another place to plant your bulb?
Child: I'll plant mine next to the sandbox.
Teacher: Put a sticker on the map to show where you will plant your bulb. Write your name under the sticker.

The teacher continued until all the children had chosen a place on the map to plant their bulbs. They wrote their names under the stickers. Some children wrote with scribbles, others with a few or all of the letters in their name.

Continue to talk with the children about where to plant their bulbs. Say to them,

> Will the bulb get enough rain? sun? Will it be protected from children running on the playground?
> Put your sticker on the space where you want to plant your bulb.
> Where did you put your sticker?

Continue until all of the children have chosen a place for their bulbs. Say to the children,

> How will you know how deeply to plant your bulb?

Show the children the package the bulbs came in and read the directions to them. Ask the children,

> How will we know that our hole is six inches deep? What is six inches?

In this study most children estimated 6 inches with their fingers; some used adding-machine tape; and one group used a ruler to mark off 6 inches on their adding-machine tape. When the children have chosen a method of showing 6 inches, take them and their map outside. Place the map on the ground in front of the children and ask them to look on the map and find the stickers showing where to plant their bulbs. Say to the children,

> Look at the map. Find your sticker and walk to the place on the playground where you plan to plant your bulb.

Allow the children, one at a time, to find the locations of their bulbs. After the children have located their places, ask them to dig holes using their markers, fill the holes with water, and cover the bulbs with soil.

ACTIVITY 5
WATCHING OUR BULBS GROW

Mathematical processes

Solving problems, keeping records, using spatial relations, and using mathematical language.

What you need

Map
Bulbs
Crayons
Paper
Polaroid camera

How you begin

The crocus bulbs will grow faster in some areas than in others. In this study they were planted in November and began to grow by the end of February. The map was used with the children in a variety of ways during the interim. One group had a treasure hunt and marked the places to look for treasure. Another group used the map to indicate where they wanted to play and where they wanted to hide their Easter eggs. Since the children used their map for a variety of activities, they often noticed their bulbs. They became very excited when they saw small green leaves. The following is the conversation between a teacher and a group of three- and four-year-olds.

Teacher:	What is happening to your bulbs?
Children:	They are green.
	Growing.
	I saw funny leaves.
Teacher:	Do all of the bulbs look the same?
Children:	No, they are some very grown and some little.
	Mine is more grown than anyone's.
Teacher:	How can you remember how your bulbs look?
Children:	Draw pictures.
	Take pictures.
	I can just remember.
Teacher:	When you go on the playground, look at the plant growing from your bulb. You can take crayons and paper outside with you to make a picture of your plant. I'll bring the Polaroid camera if you want to take pictures.

These children kept a record of their plants' growth until their flowers bloomed. The teacher allowed them to pick the flowers or leave them on the plants.

Talk with the children about their growing plants and encourage them to keep a record of their growth. Most children in this study chose to take four to six Polaroid pictures. They labeled their pictures and displayed them on the bulletin boards. The teachers encouraged the children to take a picture each time they saw a change in their plants. The bulbs were kept in the ground to multiply and grow flowers the next spring.

THOUGHTS ON MAKING MAPS

Children must have many experiences with *concrete* and *picture maps* before they are introduced to simple *base maps*. Maps were found to be appropriate for four- and five-year-olds who had had many opportunities to build and make houses and cities. They had little or no problems relating their map to the real playground. Three-year-olds enjoyed putting stickers on the map and planting bulbs but showed little interest in making the map.

Later in the spring, one teacher introduced a map of the room to the children. They divided the map into learning centers and used symbols to represent particular centers. A drawing of a book, for example, was used for the library center and a drawing of a magnifying glass for the science center. The children used the map to decide where they would play first each day. This map was as successful as the map of the playground. Children in one Head Start program had two maps—one for each group that planned together. Although the maps were the same size, the symbols used were different.

NATIONAL UNIVERSITY
LIBRARY   SAN DIEGO

ABOUT THE AUTHOR

Rosemary Althouse is a professor of early childhood education at Winthrop University, Rock Hill, South Carolina. She is also the director of the Macfeat Early Childhood Laboratory School. She earned a B.S. from the University of Pennsylvania, an M.A. from State University of Iowa, and a Ph.D. from Florida State University. Dr. Althouse has published numerous articles in professional journals and is the coauthor of *Science Experiences for Young Children* and the author of *The Young Child: Learning with Understanding* and *Investigating Science with Young Children*, all published by Teachers College Press.

NATIONAL UNIVERSITY
LIBRARY   SAN DIEGO

9425

5452